Mel Bay Presents

JACK JEZZRO: BRAZILIAN NIGHTS

A Rhythmic Musical Experience Featuring Latin Guitar

Original Compositions and Solo Improvisations by Jack Jezzro

Transcriptions and Analysis by Lenny Carlson

1 2 3 4 5 6 7 8 9 0

Table of Contents

FOREWORD

This is the second book of Jack Jezzro's original music to be published by Mel Bay. The first book, *Acoustic Dreams* (1998), presented intricate fingerstyle guitar arrangements in the "New Age Country" genre, combining elements of old-timey, modern country and sounds of the British Isles. This volume, *Brazilian Nights*, could be subtitled "and now for something completely different..." with its catchy samba rhythms and improvised (and very melodic) solos. What next, Mr. Jezzro?

That Jack plays in these and many other styles so well should come as not surprise to anyone familiar with his name as one of the mainstays of Nashville's famous recording scene. If you have not seen the first book, or don't know about Jack's background, here is some information you might find interesting. Born in West Virginia, he played piano, accordion, guitar and banjo a child. He later studied the double bass and went on to graduate from the prestigious Eastman School of Music. He moved to Nashville in 1981 after having played in the Rochester Philharmonic Orchestra for two years. He immediately won an audition and became a member of the Nashville Symphony Orchestra. During the mid-1980's he began breaking into the recording scene as both a bassist and guitarist. This "double" of guitar and bass brought him much recognition and helped establish him as one of Nashville's finest musicians. As a sideman, artist and later as a producer, he has taken part in thousands of recording sessions. His original compositions have also been heard on countless TV shows and Movies.

Jack Jezzro's compositions are often technically challenging, but always worthwhile on an aesthetic level. The originality of his "voice," his creative musical instinct and how he expresses it, is perhaps what sets Jack's music apart. He is thoroughly grounded in the academic language of music theory, but there is a melodic awareness and swing he brings that makes the listener take notice. Above all, it is sincere music, from the heart (for many musicians, their only vital organ is their wallet).

This book is a clear, simple and painless way to learn how to play and improvise melodies over standard chords in latin rhythms. The original music is very melodic, listenable and easy to follow, and Jack's execution of his musical ideas — both written and improvised — is exemplary. There is material for students on several different levels. Each piece is presented in a basic "lead sheet" version first, with the melody and some simple harmonies written along with chord symbols. If you are unsure of your chord theory, melodic execution or music reading, begin with this version. The second section of each piece is a portion of Jack's improvised solo, transcribed note-for-note off the CD, with Jack's preferred tab notation. He plays these solos accompanied by an ace group of jazz cats (yes, folks, they can groove in Nashville, too). If you are an advanced player looking for a challenge, you can work the written solo up to performance tempo and play it along with the CD. There are fills and tags that have not been included. You may also want to complete the transcription of some of these solo parts yourself. A great way to learn about music, and it will keep you awake.

I have been privileged to work with Jack Jezzro on both *Acoustic Dreams* and *Brazilian Nights*. He has distinguished himself over many years both artistically and in one of the most competitive music business environments anywhere, and has remained a down-to-earth and accessible person — quite a rarity. He's a real pro, and a good friend. I hope you benefit from our joint effort as much as we have.

LENNY CARLSON

INTRODUCTION BY JACK JEZZRO

"Brazilian Music, with it's wonderful melodies and exciting rhythms, has always been a favorite of mine to play over the years. The music of Jobim, in particular, has certainly had an influence on me and musicians all over the world. I hope that you enjoy these transcriptions of my music taken from the recording "Brazillian Nights". In addition, I want to thank the folks at Mel Bay for creating this book. I especially want to thank Lenny Carlson for his transcriptions and wonderful insight."

-Jack Jezzro

SELECTED DISCOGRAPHY

(Green Hill Recordings)

Brazilian Nights
Jazz Elegance
The Beatles on Guitar
Gershwin on Guitar
Worldbeat on Guitar
Guitar Romance
Christmas Guitar
Midnight Moon
Acoustic Dreams
Nashville Country

HOW TO USE THIS BOOK

It is assumed that the student/reader has at least several years experience as a guitarist, and knows a range of chord positions and scales. Advanced sight-reading ability is not required, but some reading facility is necessary to decipher this music on paper.

All 12 selections from Jack Jezzro's *Brazilian Nights* CD (Green Hill GHD 5112) are represented in this book. There are two sections to each piece. How best to begin?

It would be easiest and most time-efficient to start with the "lead sheet," which is a basic version of the melody along with chord symbols. Play the melody first, by itself, with a metronome. Use the tab markings as written first. Try the same tab with different fingerings to get a different sound, and then invent your own tab positions from which to play the melody. This is an excellent way to learn the neck of the guitar, and it may help you break out of any "position" ruts you may be experiencing.

After working the melody up to a reasonable tempo, look at the chord symbols. Using garden variety positions as shown in any chord dictionary, play one chord on the downbeat of each measure. Then play the melody as it fills out the rest of the measure. The idea behind this exercise is to practice shifting between harmonic/accompaniment function and melody — not as easy to do as you might think.

Your fingers function differently in block chord movement than when playing a single line: when you execute a chord, there are vertical constraints that are not relevant to single line melody playing. Also, we don't think of timbre in the same way for the two contexts. Accompaniment is not played with the same level of expression that melody is. Once you have worked with this exercise and have achieved a level of proficiency which allows you to shift smoothly at a medium tempo, try a chord-melody approach, which works best at first with simpler or slower melodies.

There are many issues we must resolve on the way to acquiring performance-level technique as chord melody-style guitarists. For example, the guitar is often thought of as a poor relative of the piano, that is to say, an instrument with harmonic and polyphonic capabilities but with an unending awkwardness in fingering that doesn't exist on a keyboard. It is perhaps more effective to conceive of the guitar as a *linear* instrument, the melodies of which can be intermittently augmented by several other voices as a block, arpeggiated chord or counterpoint. This thinking liberates us from what is essentially a negative view. It allows us to play with the natural strengths of the instrument in mind.

Harmonize portions of the melodies at first using 3rds and 6ths, and when you use fuller chord forms, try to *voice* them so that the melody note is either on top or very clearly audible. This will take a lot of experimentation on your part (surprise!). Look at the **Notation Practices** section for further ideas.

Always take small steps in your practice. Getting 1 or 2 measures correct at a slow tempo will ensure your progress much more efficiently than trying to play a passage at performance tempo immediately. **Use the metronome to build your speed, from very slow and precise up to performance tempo.** Eventually you'll be able to play along with the CD and then you can apply what you've learned to your own music.

In addition to the transcriptions, there is a page of performance notes for each piece, pointing out different keys, tempos, textures, melodic and rhythmic motives, and the relevant harmonic concepts.

Last, but very important, is how to apply the musical skills you develop here in the best way. One thing to do is to memorize as many *standards* in this style as you can, and use some of your recently acquired theory and technique on such material. Perhaps you are doing this already. Standards are songs that are part of our mainstream culture. They have achieved meaning and popularity over several generations, often because of memorable melodies, harmonies and/or lyrics. Songs like *Misty*, *Satin Doll*, *Over the Rainbow* and thousands of others are in this "best-loved" category.

Latin standards and styles that every performing jazz guitarist should study include sambas and bossas such as *Girl from Ipanema*, *Desafinado*, *One Note Samba*, *Manha de Carnaval*, *Samba de Orfeo*, *Chega de Saudade* (No More Blues), Wave, *Summer Samba*, *Brazil*, *Tico Tico*, *How Insensitive*; popular Mexican ballads like *Besame Mucho*, *Sabor a Mi* and *Somos Novios (It's Impossible)*, which are often played as a rhumba; calypsos such as *Jamaica Farewell*, *Matilda* or Sonny Rollins' *St. Thomas*; cha-chas such as *Tea for Two*, *Never on Sunday* or Charlie Parker's *My Little Suede Shoes*; tangos, guajiras, paso dobles, rancheras, corridos and other folk song and dance forms as well as U.S. standards such as *Summertime*, *The Shadow of Your Smile* and *Speak Low* that are often played in a latin rhythm.

The more you study and practice this music, the better your own music will be. Rare is the jazz performer of reputation who has not come up through many years of woodshedding the standard repertoire. Jack Jezzro has paid these dues (and a lot more) as is clearly heard in his composing and improvising.

NOTATION PRACTICES

The transcriptions in this book are in standard notation and tablature. The tablature will help you locate the notes on the neck of the guitar.

When there are several *voices* (individual parts) active, the melody is written with stems up. Because it is usually in the upper part of the staff, it is out of the way of the other voices.

The bass voice is written stems down, and is usually below the staff. The middle voice or voices may have stems that go either way, depending on the range of the parts at that point.

In order to avoid clutter, there are no right hand fingerings marked. Please see the Mel Bay Catalog for books on classical guitar technique for assistance in this area if you have questions.

There are also no dynamics (loud/soft) marked. The notation presents the skeleton of the music, leaving the nuances to you, the reader. In order to perform this music convincingly, you must listen repeatedly to the CD and develop your own sense of "touch" on each piece.

The solos are transcribed by ear, but the first section, the basic melody and chord structure, is taken from sheets written by Jack Jezzro himself. In some cases, to save time and space, or to more easily express his ideas, he wrote in common time (4/4), rather than cut time, which is often used in latin rhythm notation. Don't be concerned with the difference; the music remains the same.

The next 2 pages show notation styles that are found in the book. First there is an example of straight notation, lead-sheet style, which is largely self-explanatory, especially if you have had experience with similar books. The purpose of this page is to provide a quick review of standard musical terminology.

On the second page there are some examples of common chord-melody devices. Many guitar students have never played in this format. The basic melody used for the examples is *Mary Had a Little Lamb*, because it is universally known and can be easily retained in your musical memory as you work through the variations. Once these concepts are understood, you can apply them to your own music as well as that of Jack Jezzro.

Señor Samba

Jack Jezzro

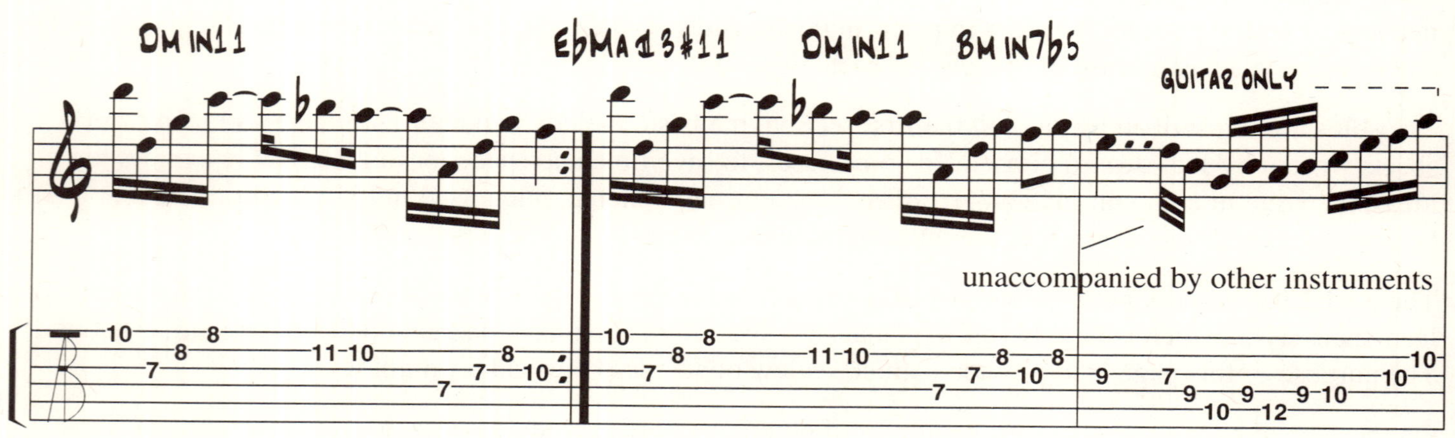

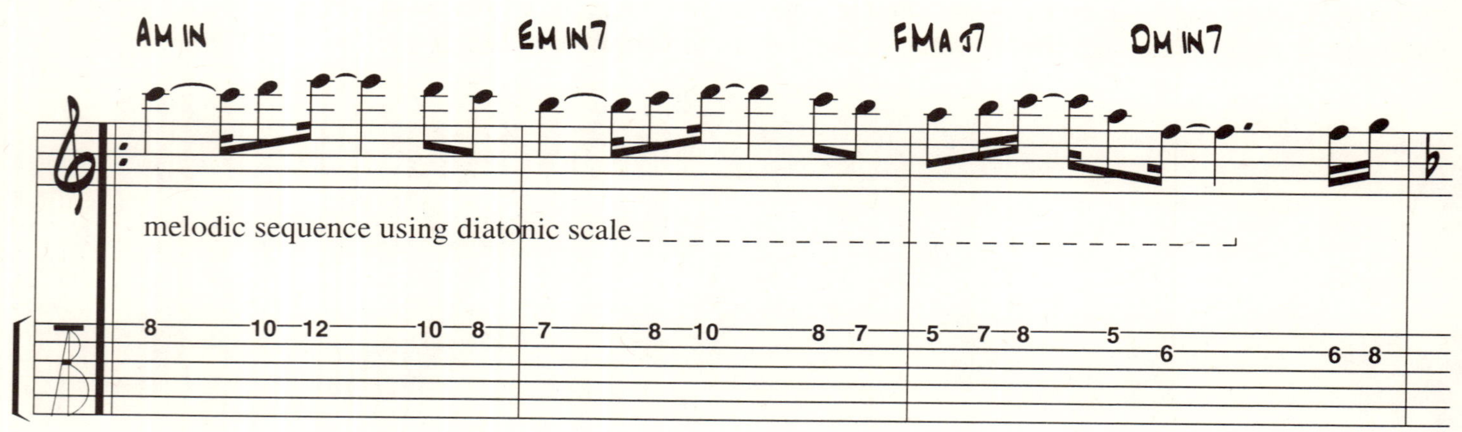

SOME COMMON CHORD-MELODY DEVICES:

PERFORMANCE NOTES

Some of the transcribed solos have been notated in cut time, and it is important to listen to the very active rhythm playing that goes on behind them. One must remember that above all this is dance music.

1. BRAZILIAN NIGHTS

Brazilian Nights is a minor melody with simple chord changes but a great deal of energy and ornamentation. Full of trills and 16th notes, it expresses a latin flavor very strongly.

The chord changes as indicated on this solo are minimal; the guitar as a solo instrument treats the 7ths, 9ths and other color tones or upper partials as melody notes, not part of the harmony.

Beginning with a minor 7th —D in the E minor chord— Jack plays a 2-measure descending figure that leads to the IV chord. Most of the solo is built around consonant chord tones, but the main ingredients here are rhythm and timbre. Notice how he varies his touch from very punchy to very legato (think about the differences in the approaches of Pat Metheny and Mahavishnu John McLaughlin). Tremendous forward motion can be sustained through the interesting use of rhythm and touch.

Another point of interest is Jack's use of open string and fretted note combinations, such as in measures 25 and 27. This is making use of the guitar in a rich and natural way, besides being helpful when making position changes.

Lastly, Jack uses space in this solo. The listener (and player) need not be overwhelmed by a constant stream of notes. It is not necessary to make history in 32 bars.

2. FIESTA ESPANOL

This brisk offering is again in minor mode, but the changes come a bit quicker, at about one per measure.

Fiesta Espanol is set in a more remote key than is *Brazilian Nights*. F♯ minor is relative to A major, a very guitar-friendly key with many notes available to be played on open strings. However, the chord *C♯7* contains the third *e♯* forcing us to alter the overall position and approach.

In the exposition of the melody, Jack uses double-stops with the 6th interval (mm. 6-8, 13-14) to contrast with his scale runs. Along with its inversion the 3rd, it is the most commonly used interval, very consonant and easy on the ears. Taken together, the two can be used to harmonize most melodies effectively. Harmony provides background and support; the larger character of the music, whether sweet, percussive or far out, is usually best expressed by the melody. Thus it is not always necessary to have dissonant harmonies to be adventurous musically.

Remember that the natural minor, which is identical to the major scale, is often used in descending patterns in latin flavor-music. In the entire solo transcription the melodic note *e♯* is played only in measures 23 and 29. One can draw a comparison between this tonality and that of the blues, which uses pentatonic scales and develops tension between the flatted third and the natural third.

At m.17, Jack plays a 4-bar sequence of quarter-note triplets that express the harmonic movement. Don't be afraid to play something repetitive like this. Both player and listener need something to hang on to. Devices such as melodic sequences give your solo unity and provide a platform from which you can jump off in a flight of technical wizardry.

3. SENOR SAMBA

This selection may remind you of some of Chick Corea's music, flitting about and coming to rest in surprising places. The two chords of the introduction fit into the B♭ Major scale, with the 4th intervals setting up a modern sound and a lot of rhythmic tension. The line is played very percussively, with some notes "ghosted." This is a jazz technique in which some melody notes are not played — almost swallowed — but the overall flow of the line implies these notes and carries the weight. Besides working with this recording, listen to the improvisations of guitarist Jim Hall or any master sax player like Charlie Parker for further examples of ghosted notes.

The *guitar only* phrase at measure 7 is an example of very fast fingerstyle playing. Such a phrase cannot be as easily executed with a flat pick. Another extremely important factor in the execution of this music is left hand fingering. In some cases it is more efficient to stretch your LH fingers along one string (horizontally) than in one vertical position across the strings. The music will dictate this to you. There are no rules for fingering beyond "whatever works."

There is a lot of rhythmic variety in this piece, and a good chance to practice syncopated figures within 16th note patterns. The solo itself is short, only 16 measures long, in cut-time. The melodic ideas in the improvised solo are largely based on the chords and scales related to them. Of particular interest is the half-note triplet phrase (mm. 10-13), which utilizes both rhythmic and melodic syncopation to excellent effect.

4. LEBLON

The first 16 bars of Leblon are the Introduction. This section provides a textbook example of a iv - v - i resolution and different melodies that can be associated with it.

The verse (m. 17) begins on *Fmaj7*, which is the chord built on the flatted 6th in A minor. Compare this with the *iv* (*D minor*) and the *ii* (*Bmin7♭5*). *Fmaj7* includes F, A, C and E. *Dmin9* includes: D, F, A, C and E. *Bmin7♭5* includes B, D, F and A. All of these chords are made up of scale tones, with no accidentals beyond that of the original key. They each can resolve to *E7*(with a *♭9* or *♭5*) on the way to the tonic, but there is a different sound with each type of resolution.

The most direct — strongest — resolution is from the *ii*, while the most remote is from the *♭vi*. Remember that in this case stronger is not always better. A song like *Happy Birthday* has a strong and obvious chord progression. When a composer or improvisor is dealing with more subtle sounds (think Claude Debussy, Bill Evans or countless other modern musicians), a different, more indirect approach is needed.

The guitar solo begins at m. 67 in Leblon, so it is not a separate selection. You might want to address measure 65 as well.It is all double stops, played on the 2nd/3rd strings. On a nylon string guitar the top three strings are unwound, thus allowing for a silent and smooth transition between these positions. In this style, as with most jazz and classical music for guitar, there is a premium placed on "effortless" movement between positions.

The apparent lack of effort comes only with practice and planning, however. The fingers must be planted in the target position with precision timing and a minimum of motion. Play the first quarter note (A & C) with your first two fingers; play the third quarter (B & D) with fingers 3 and 4. Practice this measure over and over, holding each note to the end of its value. Begin very slowly, working with a metronome set at 60 and increasing incrementally to 200. Then do this exercise an octave down, an octave up, in different keys and in major. This kind of isolation of a particular figure is an excellent way to practice. You will learn more about the neck of the guitar and greatly increase your technical facility in the process.

5. PAQUETA, ISLE OF LOVE

Paqueta is a lush and romantic piece, set in a slow 4/4 tempo. There is much ornamentation in the basic melody, such as trills and slurs. These phrasing effects have a completely different sound when performed at faster tempos.

The melodic motive is visible from the first measure (at the sign): a 4th interval down, a 3rd up and a 2nd down. The pattern is altered to make a pickup to the *Amin9* chord at m.7. The way in which this little figure is woven through the various harmonies that follow is what gives the piece unity and beauty.

Measures 13-16 present an example of what the motive sounds like with a *ii -V* (*F♯m7♭5 - B7+5*) background, rather than the original *i - iv* (*Emin - Amin*). Compare the sounds of the chords. *A minor* with an added 6th is an inversion of *F♯m7♭5*. These chords, along with *B7*, can be thought of as movement or tension chords, while *E minor* is a chord of resolution both in this key and in its relative key, G major.

The resolution to *Cmaj7* in measure 15 is *deceptive*, a musical term which states the obvious: the listener is expecting something else. Deceptive cadences often develop into new, different and pleasing sections of a particular piece of music.

The solo is 16 measures long, plus the pickup. Because of the slow tempo, the embellishments and improvisation in general usually involves complex rhythmic figures, such as triplets and sixteenths. There are a number of interesting musical devices Jack Jezzro uses in his improvisation here, including 16ths followed by longer tones or triplets and ascending/ descending melody lines with a wide range. Perhaps most challenging for the student are the large interval leaps when combined with 16ths. Jack has a particular way of fingering these passages to facilitate them, as do all accomplished guitarists. Efficient and musically appropriate fingering is vital to the execution of any music. It takes years of listening and experimentation to solve these problems. The best thing, of course, is to relax and enjoy the journey, if possible.

6. CAFE CALYPSO

Cafe Calypso is notable for it's beautiful melody and imaginative use of quarter-note triplets. Like any specific rhythmic figure, triplets can be overdone to the point where they become stale and "old-hat." The trick is to use these figures with variety. An examination of the original melody and Jack's improvised solo bears out how important such variety is to successful musical thinking.

Set in the key of D Major, the melody (at the sign) begins on the *vi*, going next to the *iii* and then to the IV. Look at the bass notes A and F♯ in the chords with slashes. These chords are played in their 1st inversion, with the 3rd — as opposed to the root — in the bass. Voice-leading in the bass can be a source of variety as well, and can sustain listener interest where root position chords alone might fail to do so.

In addition to the rhythm figures in the solo, look at the texture in the different measures. Beginning with double stops over Gmin7, Jack plays syncopated staccato note (m. 3), a trill in m.4 and a thicker chordal passage (mm. 5-7). Many players with great facility neglect the *musical* aspect of the solo, preferring to dazzle with lick-based pyrotechnics. Jack has this facility, but prefers to use it in the service of the music. His solos on this CD are very thoughtful andf melodic, if a bit challenging to the student-reader.

7. LATIN STORM

Played at a quick tempo, *Latin Storm* presents some technical challenges in the exposition of the melody. Listen carefully to the recording to get the rhythms and phrasing correct.

The key of D minor is friendly to the guitar, except in the use of the subdominant *G minor*. The tonic chord has open strings that can resonate, and the dominant is our old friend A7. Beware of shifts to G minor which necessitate using your fingers to barre in a different configuration. The "cleanest" players in the jazz chord melody style have a minimum of string noise that can be heard in the shift. You must listen critically to become aware of this phenomenon. [The first time I really listened to the string noise I was making it was quite an unhappy revelation — LC]

The solo is notated in cut-time. Jack Jezzro gives the impression of gliding or lightly touching the top of the rhythm in pieces like this. It is a satisfying and altogether musical experience.

The chord *B♭Maj7♯11* has as its components B♭ - F - A - D - E when positioned at the 1st fret and including the open high E. In certain voicings the 5th (F) may be cut out and the 9th (C) included. The chord components all come from the F major — and D natural — minor scale, so even with a complicated name and symbol you can still keep your thinking simple. Compare this chord with *Emin7♭5*, which contains E - G - B♭ - D. Many melodic phrases can be played over the two chords interchangeably. The difference is one of harmonic function, with the E minor chord being a ii7 and moving through A7 on its way to D minor, and the B♭ chord being a subdominant (IV chord) in F major.

8. MIRANDA

This selection is set at medium tempo. It is in the key of E minor. The 16-measure solo is transcribed as part of the original melody; it is not in a separate section.

Jack Jezzro uses open strings both for their sound (which differs from that of the fretted notes) and as an aid to position change. A good example of the latter is mm. 47-48, in which the open B string is followed by the high D, an upward leap of a 10th. Using the open string at the end of a lower register passage is a proven way of making such a large leap successfully. Use whatever works for you, but combining logical fingering plus intelligent use of open strings ensures execution of passages that in "real time" pass by all too quickly.

9. THE ROAD TO PONTA PORA

Set in the key of B♭ Major, the second chord of the 4-measure Introduction is *E♭min6/F*. What does this mean? Ebmin6 is, after all, the first inversion of *Cmin7♭5* (check it out, folks) and the */F* indicates a bass note. Sometimes the slash can indicate two triads or other chordal configurations against each other, forming a bitonal or polytonal cluster.

In this case, the E♭min6 actually functions literally, as a minor built on the IV. The sound of a minor 6th chord is unique, with a sense of resolution (unlike a minor 7th or a dominant 7th) and a beautiful, transparent quality. It is a sound long associated with Brazilian music.

Note the modulations in the melody (B♭ to G♭ to D to E♭). The line weaves in and out of the keys by adding accidentals and small transitional figures.

The solo section is divided into two parts. The first is an 8-measure solo that takes us up to the first modulation (G♭). This move is a standard one in jazz and classical music, to a third-related key. Think B♭ - G, B♭ - D♭, B♭ -D. There are common tones that the third-related key shares with the original. Rather than *Cmin7 - F7 - B♭Maj7*, you can play *Cmin7 - F7 - G♭Maj7*. As always, you must experiment with these progressions until they make musical sense to you.

The second section is the Fade Out at the end. The chords are I -iv6 as in the Introduction, and Jack Jezzro plays lightly and in a relaxed manner over the repeated pattern. Another word for this type of progression is vamp.

10. LADRON DE CORAZON

This selection is in a different format, with no guitar solo. The Spanish title translates to "Tears of the Heart," and it was composed and arranged by Jack Jezzro's friend (and fellow Nashville studio whiz) Chris McDonald. The flute and piano both solo very melodically over the chord changes, which are included in the transcription.

The guitar part is quite active, however. At measure 9, the guitar and flute play the melody in octaves. Observe the staccato markings, and listen to the sharp attack on those particular notes. The melody provides a good study in the contrast between short and longer tones.

In the second ending there is a short phrase of 16th notes. This could be played in first position, except that the next measure (16) has a note at the 8th fret. A good guideline regarding position playing is the range of the passage, what came before, and what comes next. Other items of concern in the playing of the melody include the double-stops in m. 19 (played on the 2nd/3rd strings) and the sextuplets in m. 24.

Ladron de Corazon was taken directly from Chris McDonald's arrangement. Jack uses certain slurs and other phrasing devices that are not notated. Careful listening to the performance on the recording will resolve any questions you may have about how to finger or phrase which notes.

11. THE BEACH AT IPANEMA

This is an extremely melodic piece, set at a moderate tempo. Not too many mysteries here, just beautiful music executed very well.

One spot to consider: measure 8 of the solo. Jack is not making reference to the ♭5 in his melodic improvisation; a *G natural* note is set against the chord. How does this work? It works because there are several *registers* and *timbres* functioning at once. The bass voice (and attached harmonies) is clearly resolving downward by half-steps to *Fmaj7* (the IV — subdominant chord) at the beginning of measure 9, while the melody is being played elsewhere, developing according to its own logic. As long as there is integrity (strength and direction) in each part, these different components of the music can peacefully coexist. Such *dissonance* is what makes music like this interesting to listen to and to perform.

12. MIDNIGHT IN RIO

This is a lively way to end the book. The melody (section 1.) of *Midnight in Rio* was taken directly from a lead sheet by Jack himself. It is written in common time (4/4), and there are a number of 16th note figures that will take some study.

The solo is notated in cut-time. The rhythm feel is definitely in 2, and this format is much easier to read at slower practice tempos. From measures 7 - 13, Jack develops a very interesting and challenging syncopated figure. This will take repeated listening to understand. Throughout the 2nd half of the solo he uses the chord solo approach that was briefly addressed in the previous *Notation* pages. This is one of many aspects of guitar playing that takes years to perfect, but once a student has this facility, the rewards are great. Just witness the wonderful music that Jack Jezzro has made on this CD.

This page has been left blank to avoid awkward page turns.

Brazilian Nights
Jack Jezzro
Emin Emin9 Emin Emin Emin9 Amin7
Amin7 Amin13 B7 Emin
Guitar only
Amin7 B7 Emin
Cmaj7 Amin9 B7 Emin

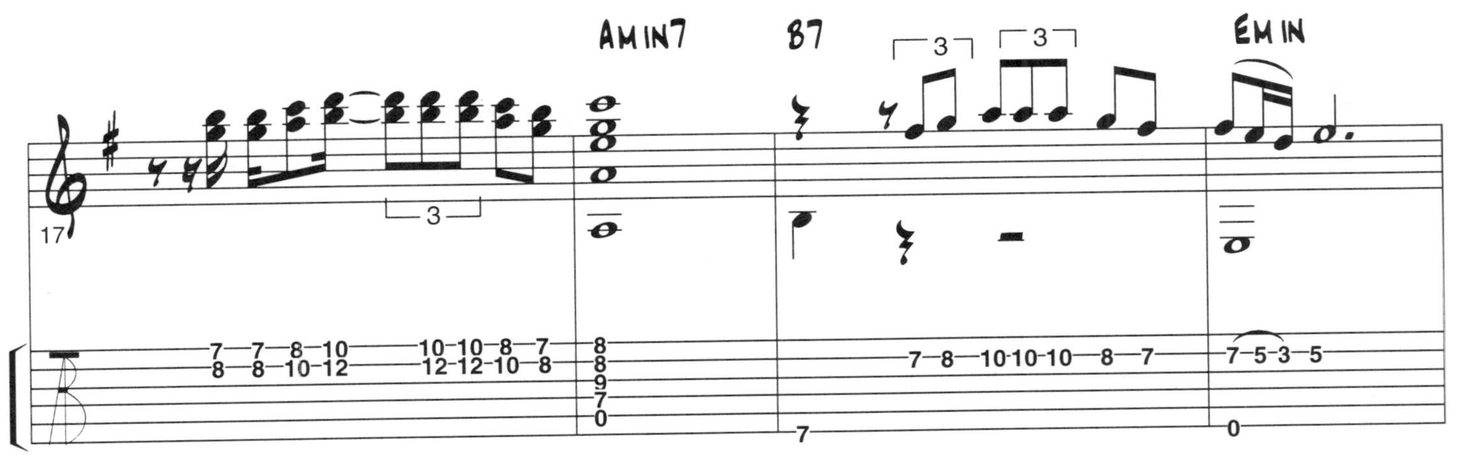
AMIN7
B7
EMIN

CMAJ9
CONTINUE SIMILE ACCOMPANIMENT
AMIN9
B7
EMIN

AMIN
AM(MAJ7)
AMIN7
AMIN6
EMIN
EMIN9
EMIN

AMIN
AM(MAJ7)
AMIN7
AMIN6
B7
B7#5

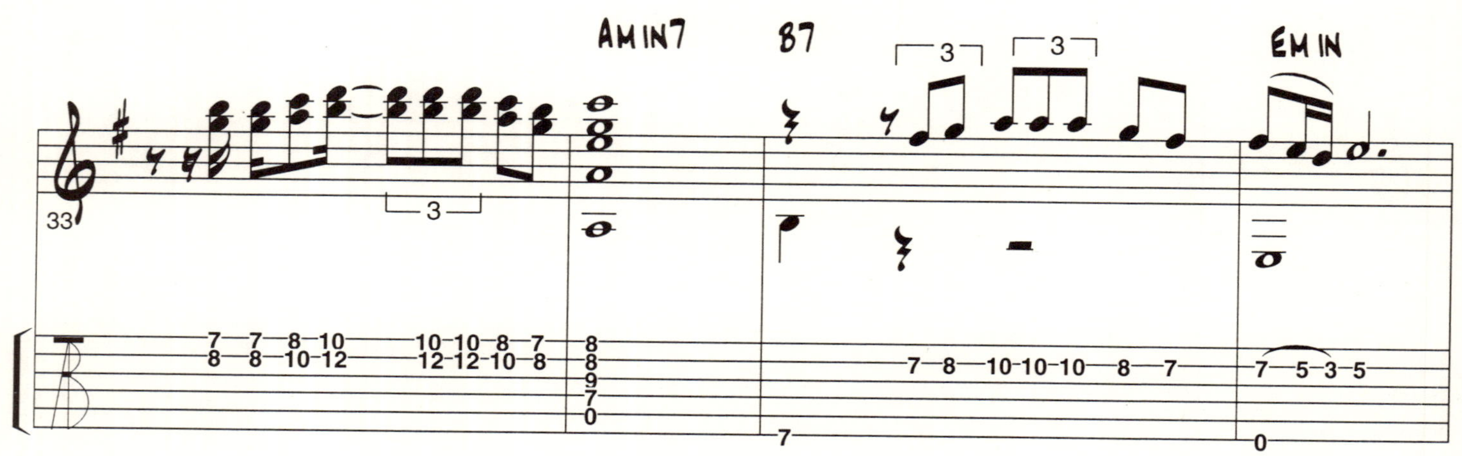
AMIN7
B7
EMIN
33

CMAJ9
AMIN9
B7
tr
EMIN
37

B7
(B7)
tr
EMIN
41

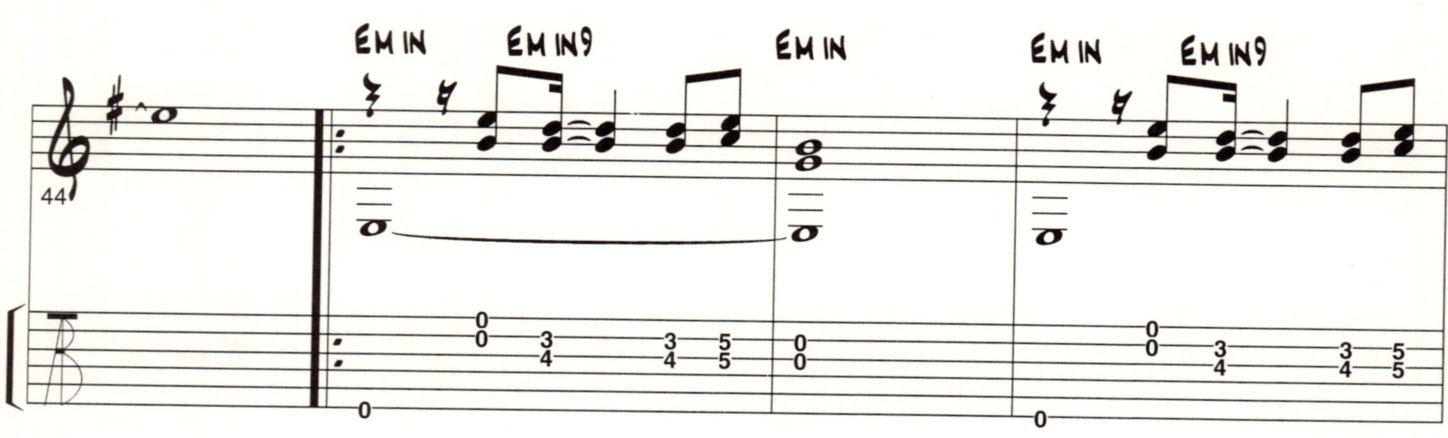
EMIN
EMIN9
EMIN
EMIN
EMIN9
44

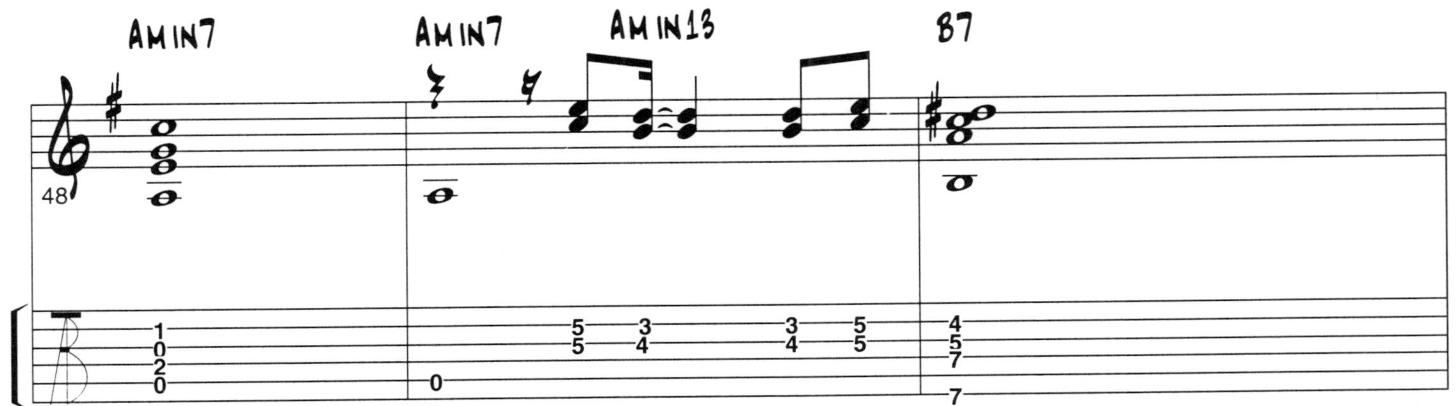
AMIN7
AMIN7
AMIN13
B7
48
1
0
2
0
0
5
5
3
4
3
4
5
5
4
5
7
7

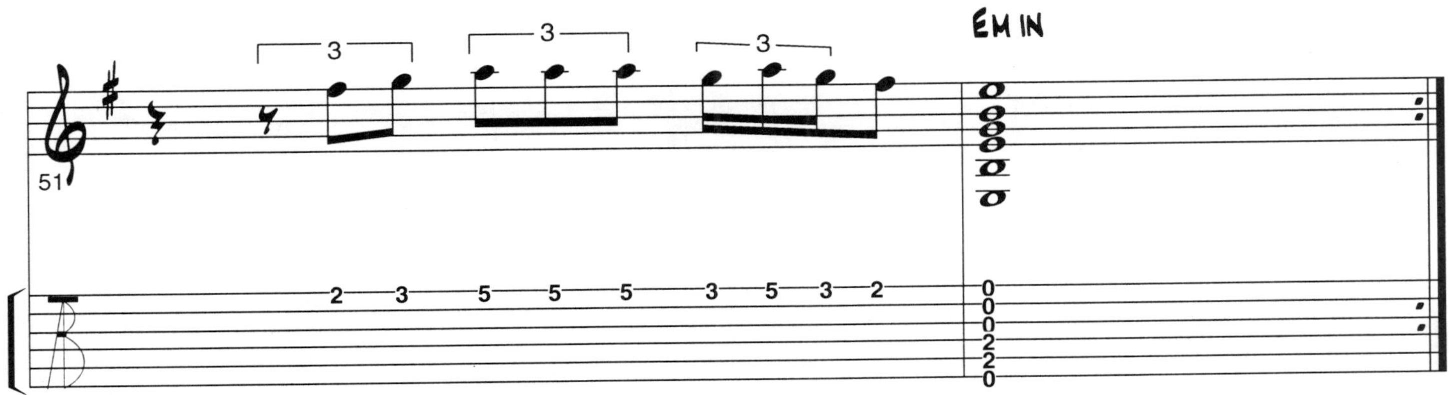
EMIN
3
3
3
51
2
3
5
5
5
3
5
3
2
0
0
0
2
2
0

Brazilian Nights: Solo

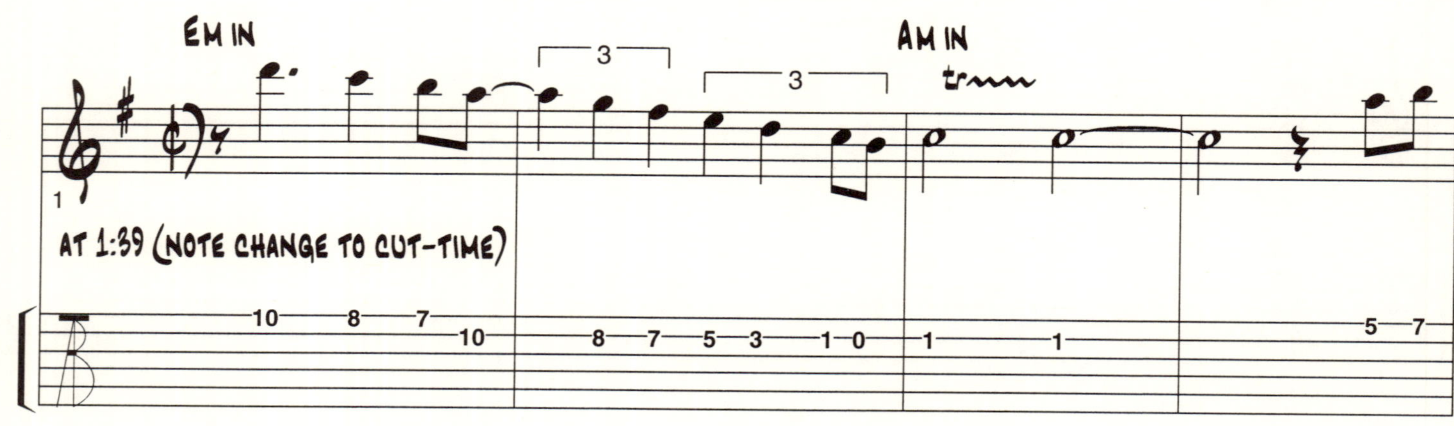

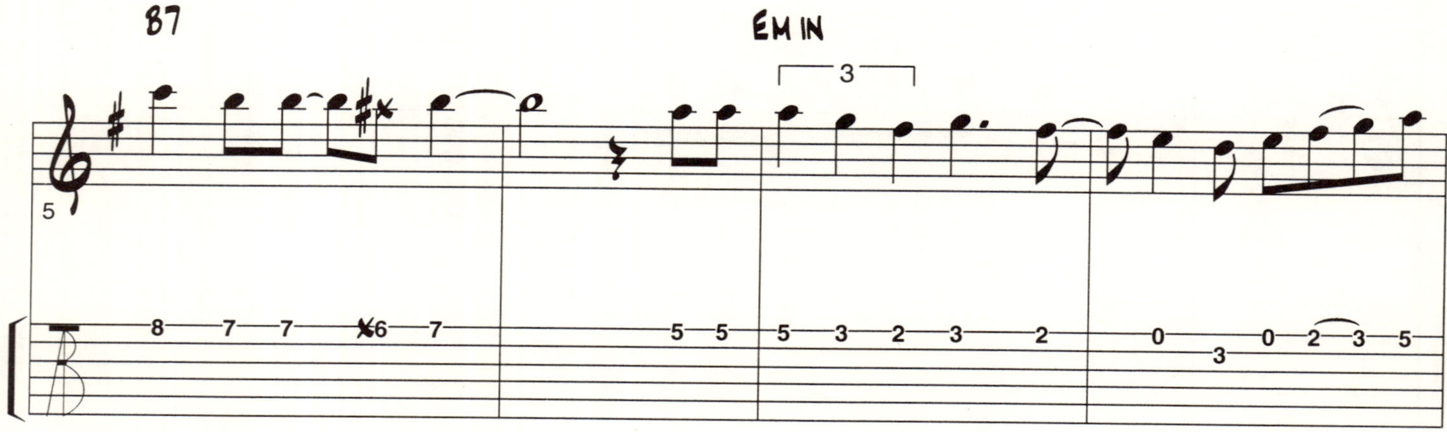

16

AMIN
B7
19

EMIN
22

AMIN
B7
25

3
3
tr
EM IN
28
8
7
10
8
7
7
7
5
8
7
5

(PIANO SOLO)
31
5
3
3
1
1
0
0
2

This page has been left blank to avoid awkward page turns.

Fiesta Espanol

Jack Jezzro

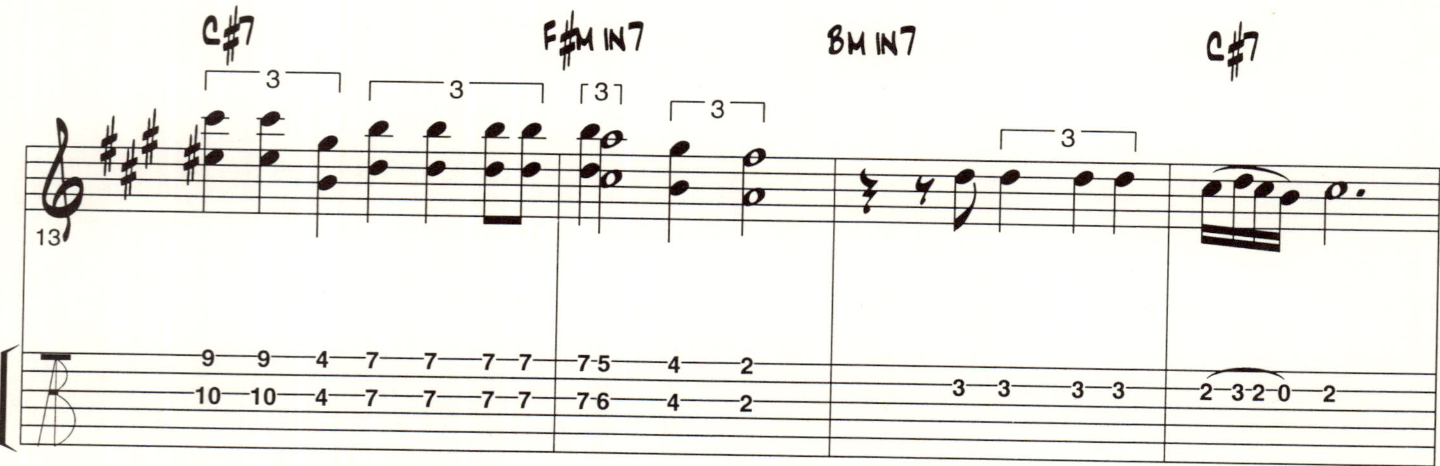

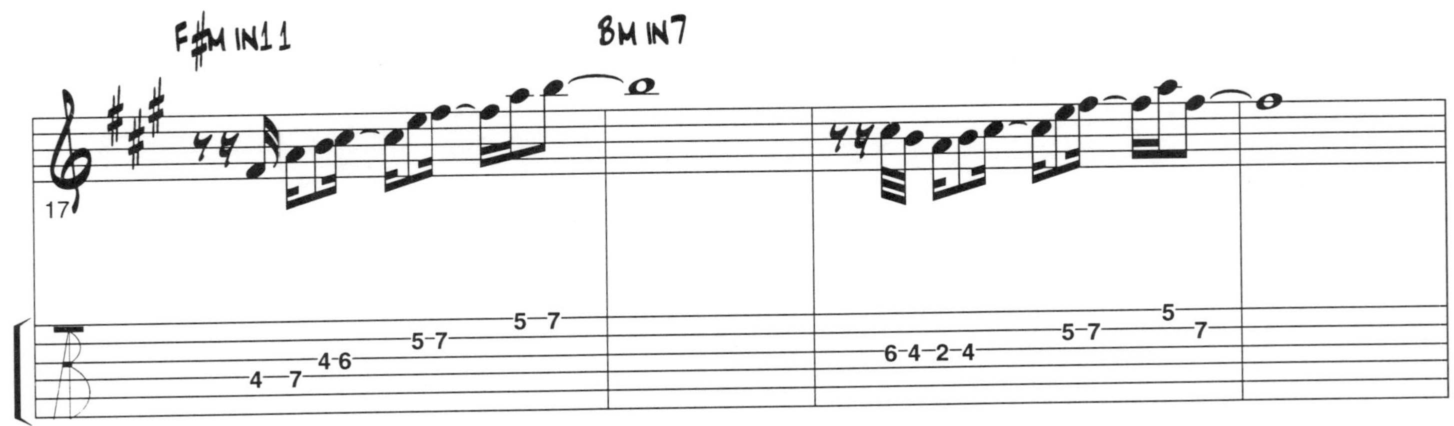
F#MIN11
BMIN7
17

C#7
F#MIN7
BMIN7
BMIN+7
F#MIN7
21

A
E7
BMIN7
F#MIN7
E7
25

A
E7
BMIN7
C#7
29

BMIN7
F#MIN7
BMIN7
C#7
3
33

DMAJ7
BMIN7
C#7
F#MIN7
3
37

CHORDS FOR GUITAR SOLO
F#MIN7
BMIN7
F#MIN7
SIMILE RHYTHM ACCOMP.
C#7
41

BMIN7
F#MIN7
C#7
F#MIN7
45
D.S. AL CODA

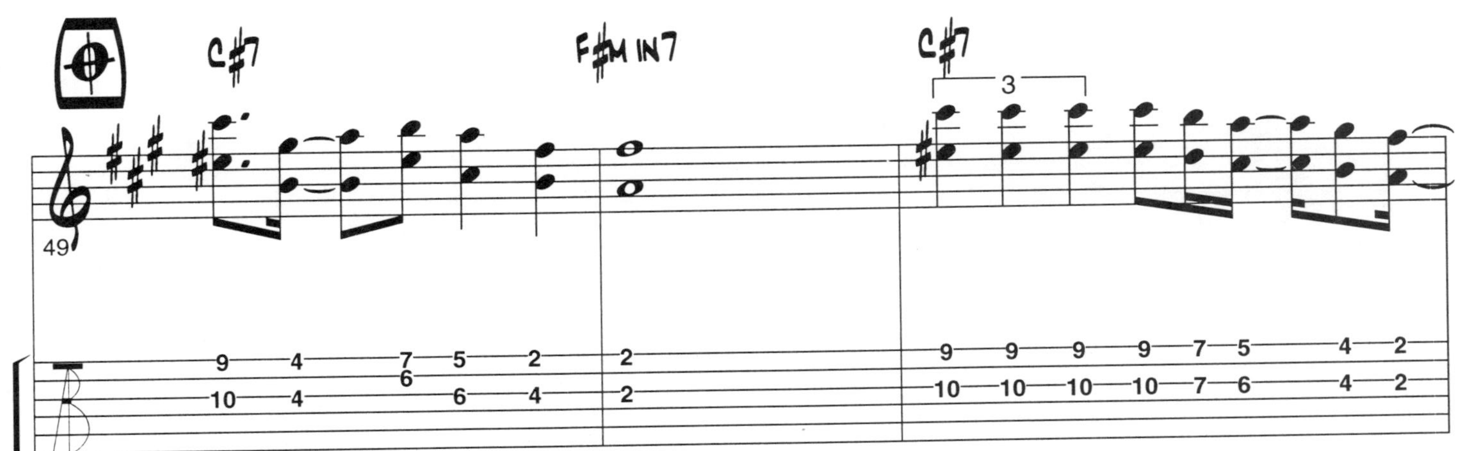
C#7
F#MIN7
C#7
3
49

F#MIN7
C#7
F#MIN7
52

Fiesta Espanol: Solo

Jack Jezzro

BMIN7
F#MIN7
C#7
F#MIN7
C#7
BMIN7
F#MIN7
PIANO SOLO
C#7
F#MIN7

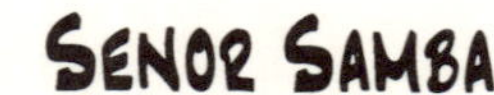
SENOR SAMBA

JACK JEZZRO

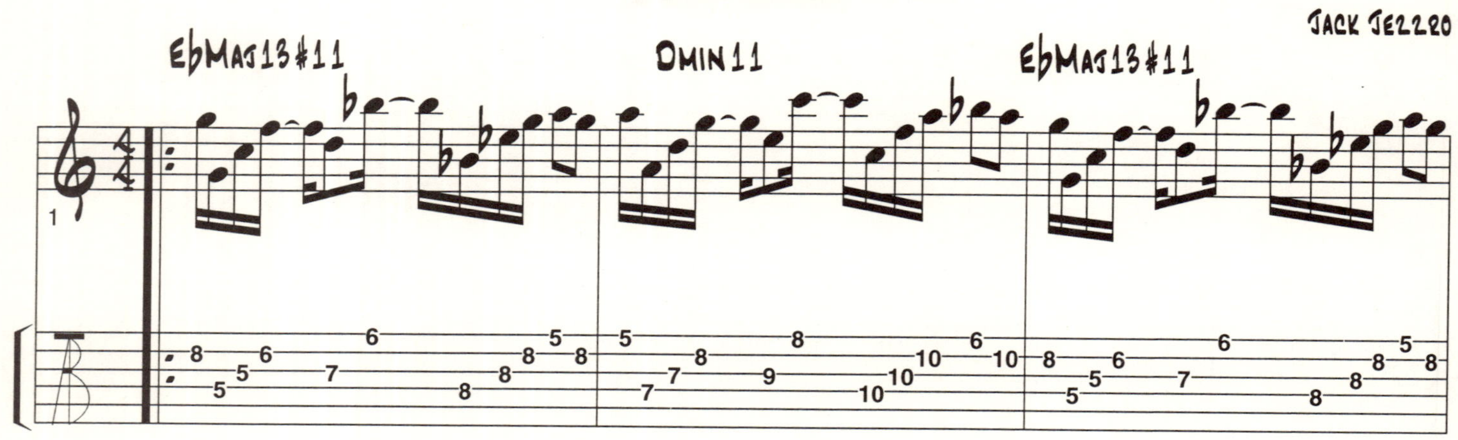
E♭MAJ13#11
DMIN11
E♭MAJ13#11

DMIN11
E♭MAJ13#11
DMIN11
BM7♭5
GUITAR ONLY

AMIN
EMIN7
FMAJ7
DMIN7

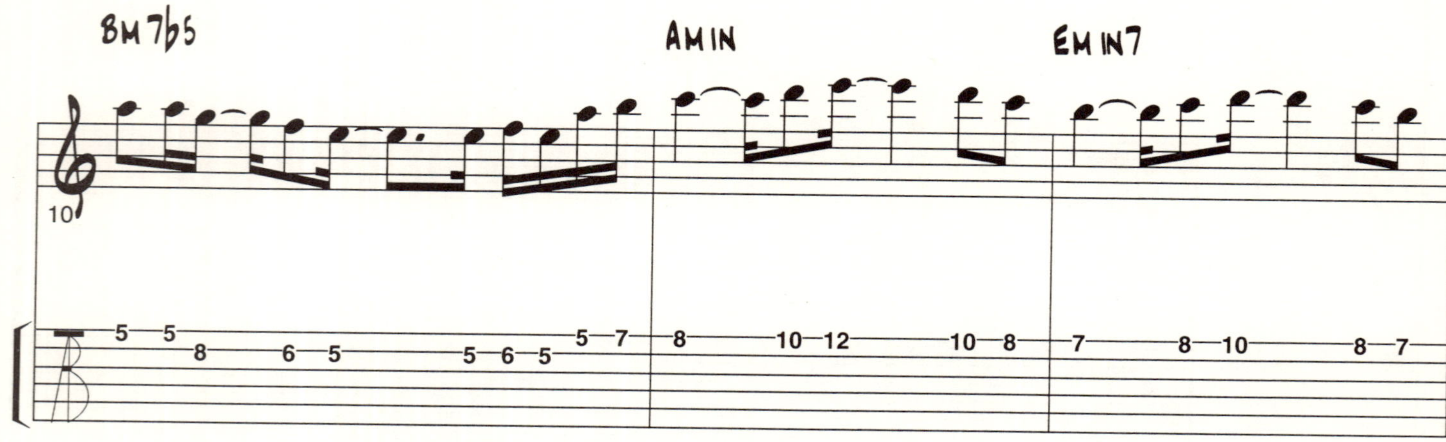
BM7♭5
AMIN
EMIN7

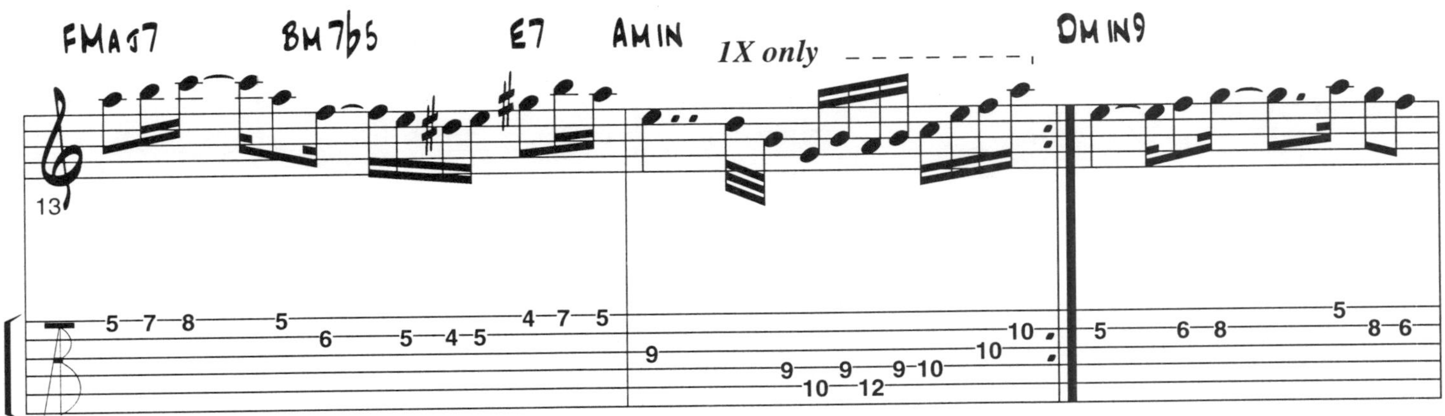
FMAJ7
BM7b5
E7
AMIN
1X only
DMIN9

AMIN7

DMIN9
AMIN7

EbMIN9

B♭MIN7
E♭MIN9
25
6 7 9 6 9 7
6 7 9 6 9
6 7 9 6 9 7

DMIN7
BM7♭5
E7+5
28
6 7 9 6 9
6 5 6 8 6 5
9 10 9 12 9 10 10 10

AMIN
EMIN7
FMAJ7
DMIN7
31
8 10 12 10 8
7 8 10 8 7
5 7 8 5 6 6 8
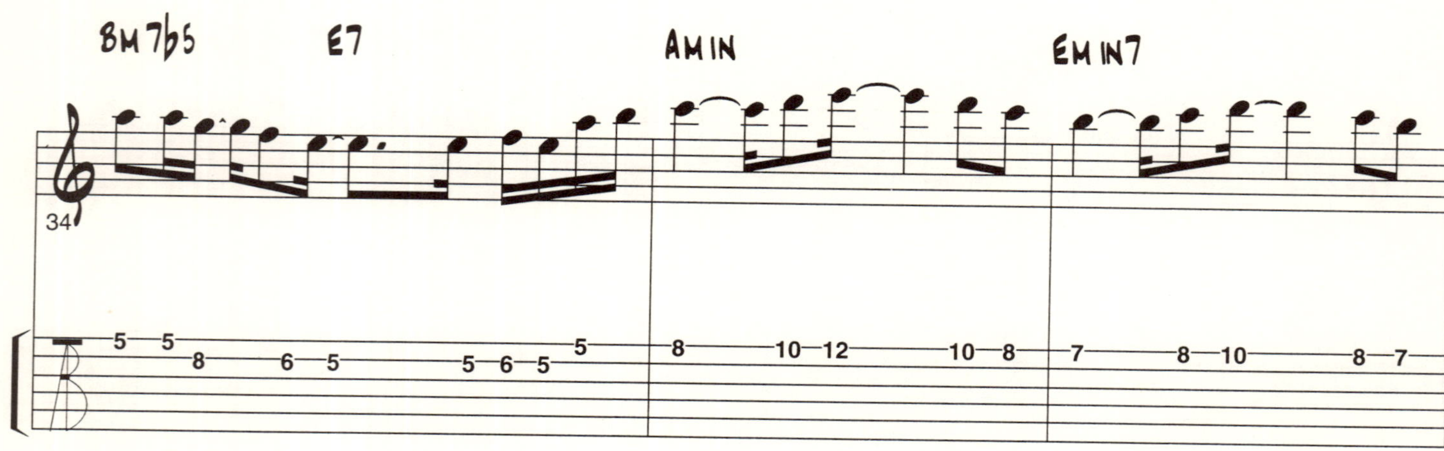
BM7♭5
E7
AMIN
EMIN7
34
5 5 8 6 5 5 6 5 5
8 10 12 10 8
7 8 10 8 7

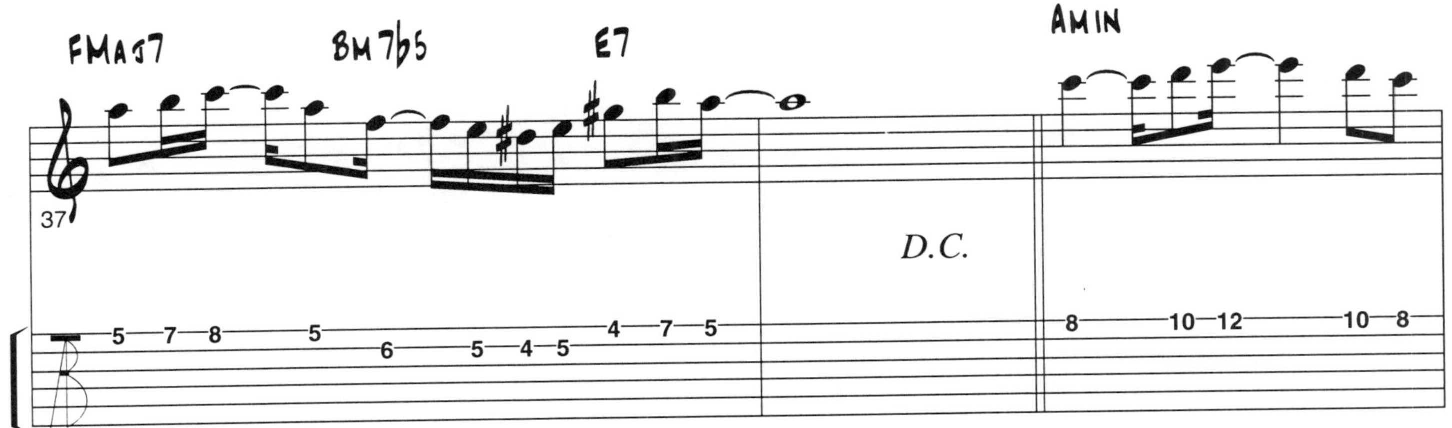
FMAJ7
BM7b5
E7
AMIN
37
D.C.

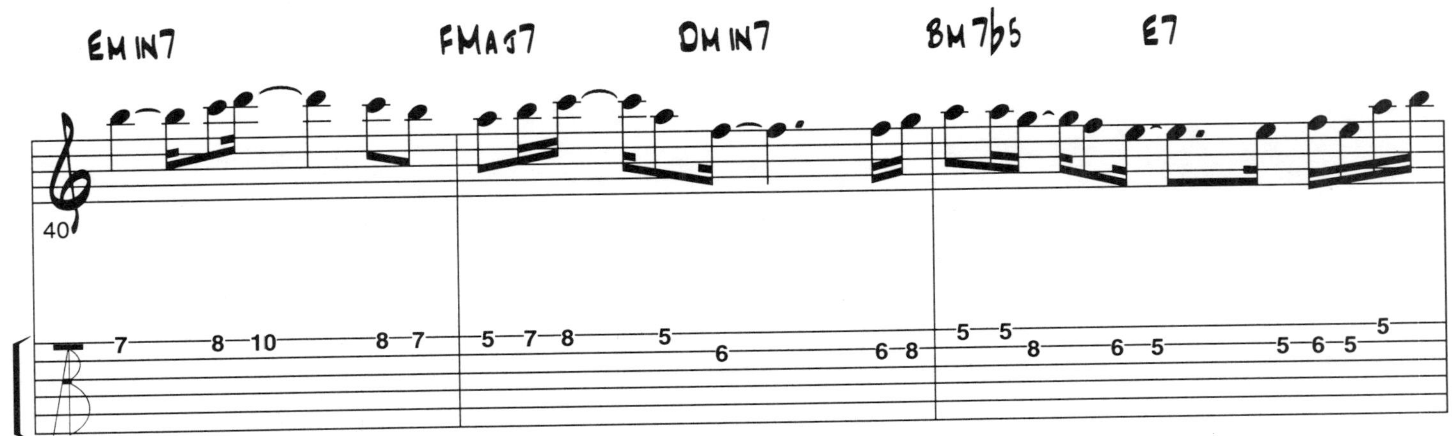
EMIN7
FMAJ7
DMIN7
BM7b5
E7
40

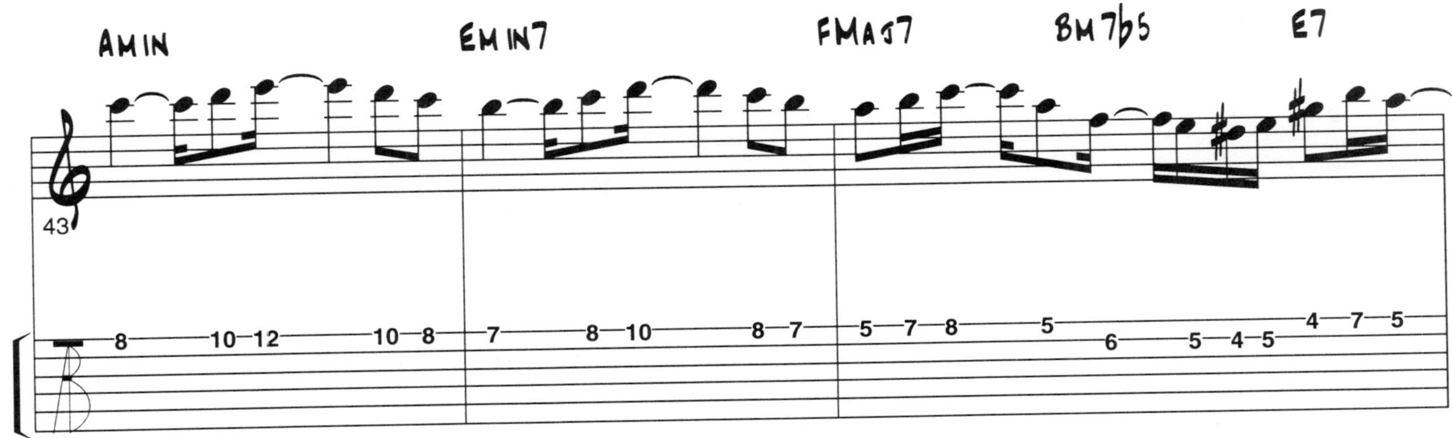
AMIN
EMIN7
FMAJ7
BM7b5
E7
43

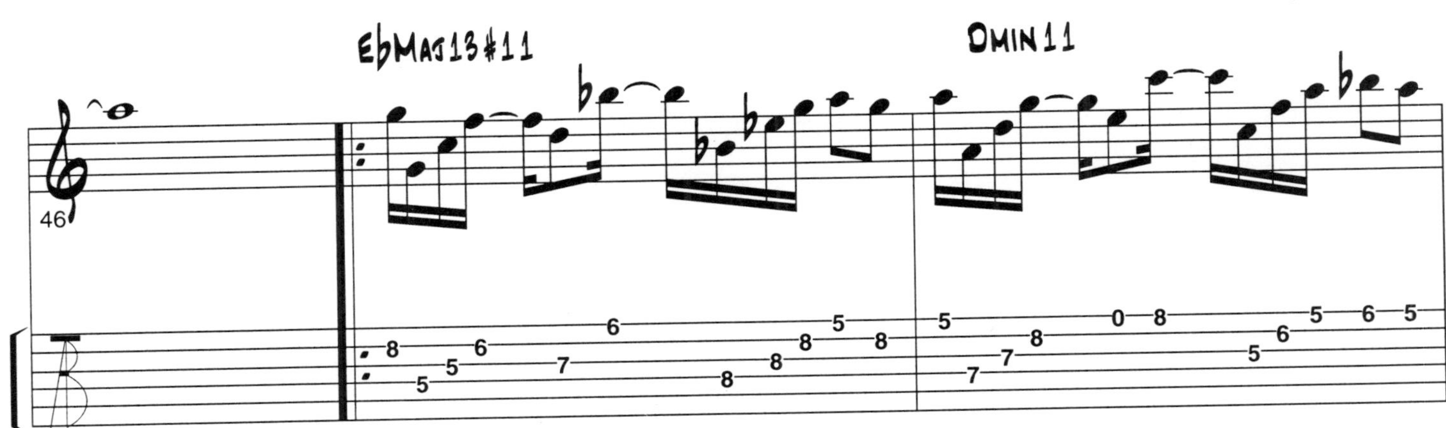
EbMAJ13#11
DMIN11
46

E♭MAJ13#11
DMIN11
49

E♭MAJ13#11
DMIN11
BM7♭5
E7+5
51

AMIN7
BM7♭5
E7+5
AMIN
53

SENOR SAMBA: SOLO

JACK JEZZRO

(AT 1:57; NOTE CHANGE TO CUT-TIME)

AMIN7
BM7b5

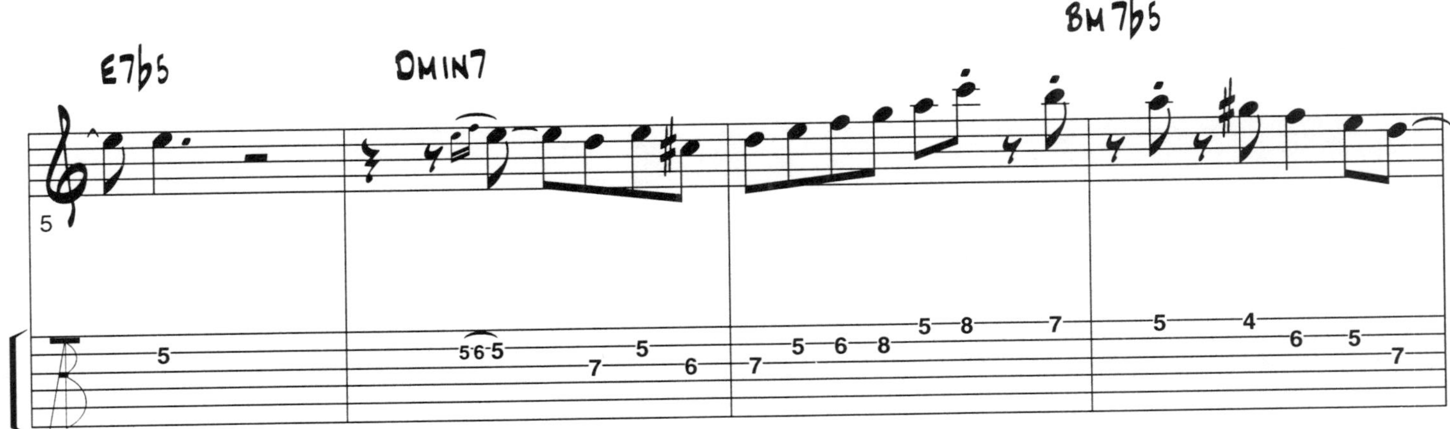
E7b5
DMIN7
BM7b5

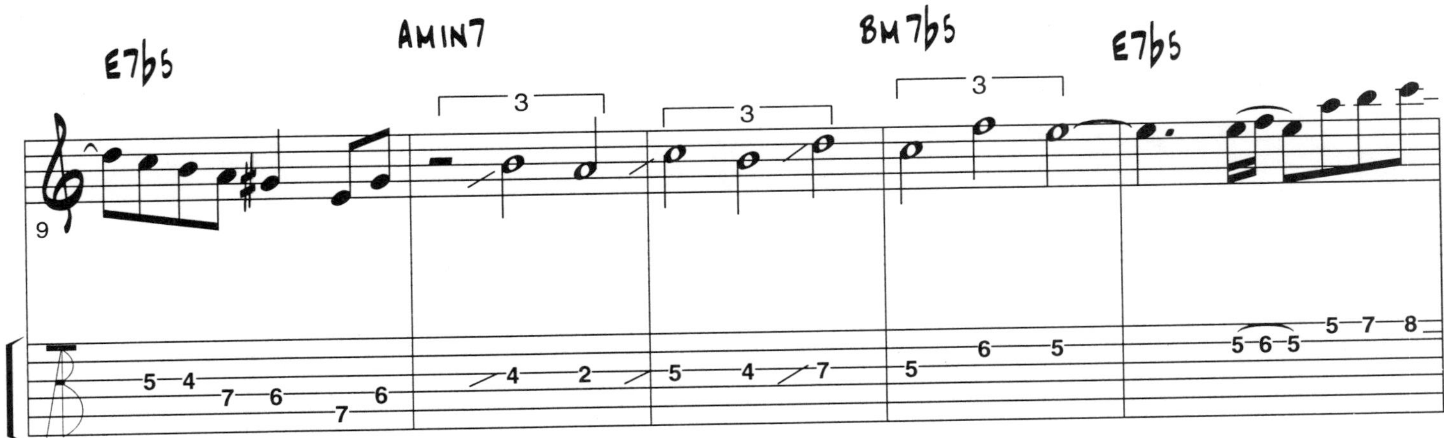
E7b5
AMIN7
BM7b5
E7b5

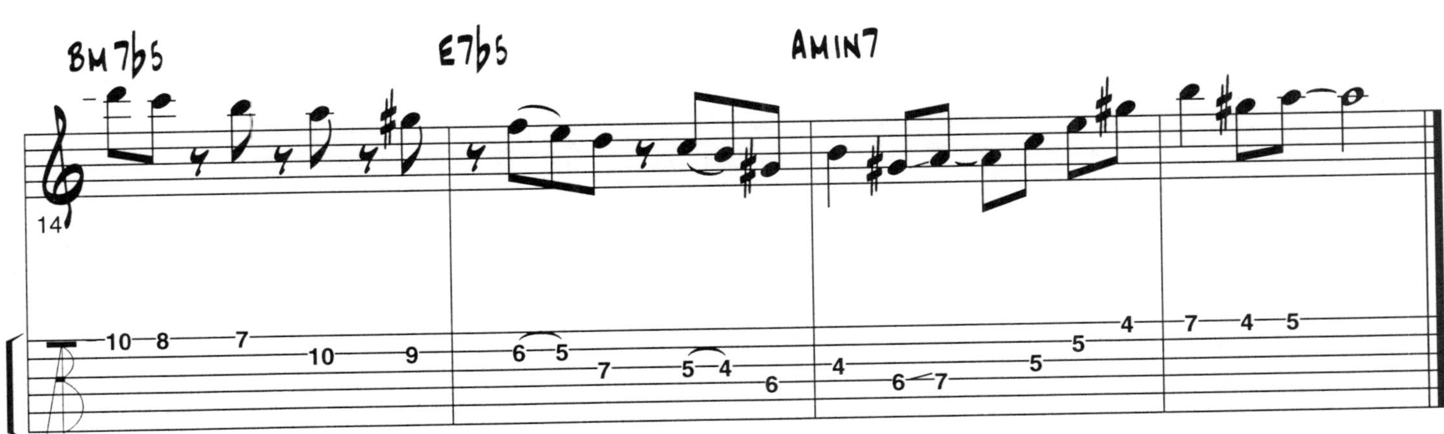
BM7b5
E7b5
AMIN7

Leblon

Jack Jezzro

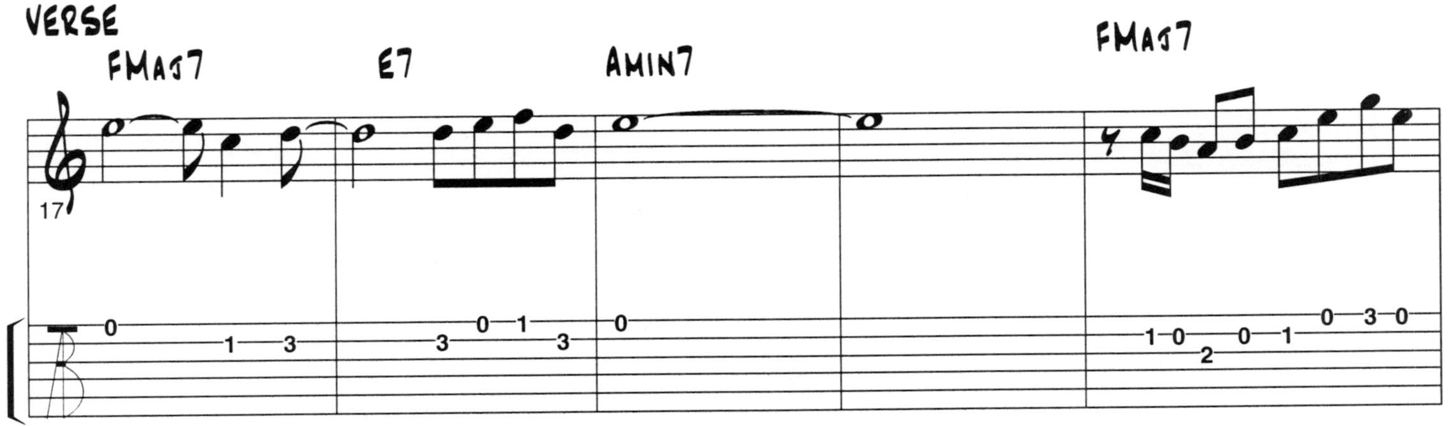
VERSE
FMAJ7
E7
AMIN7
FMAJ7
17

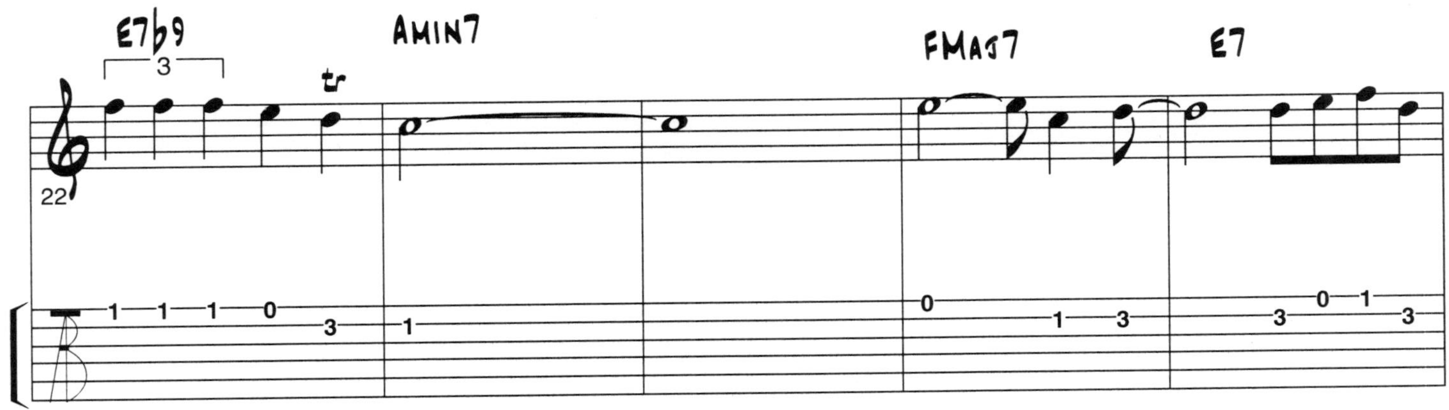
E7♭9
AMIN7
FMAJ7
E7
22

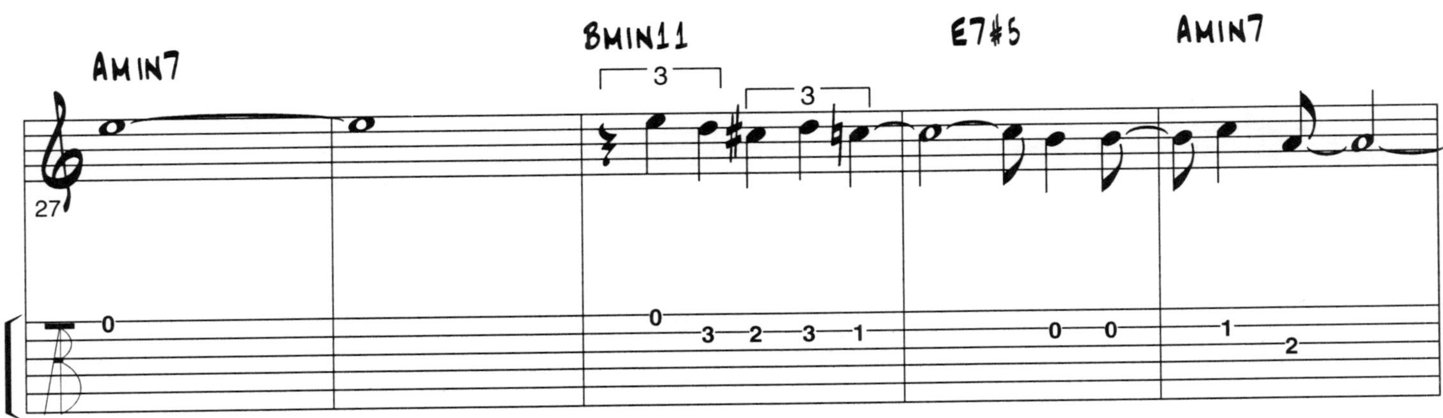
AMIN7
BMIN11
E7♯5
AMIN7
27

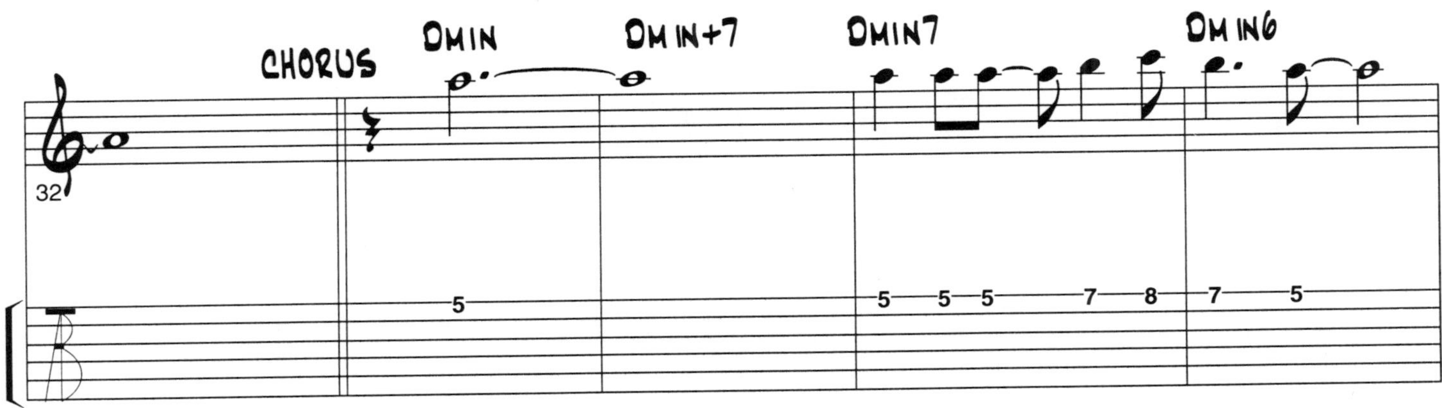
CHORUS
DMIN
DMIN+7
DMIN7
DMIN6
32

AMIN7
E7♭9
AMIN7
DMIN
37

DMIN+7
DMIN7
DMIN6
BMIN11
42

E7♭9
FMAJ7
E7
AMIN7
47

FMAJ7
E7♭9
AMIN7
52

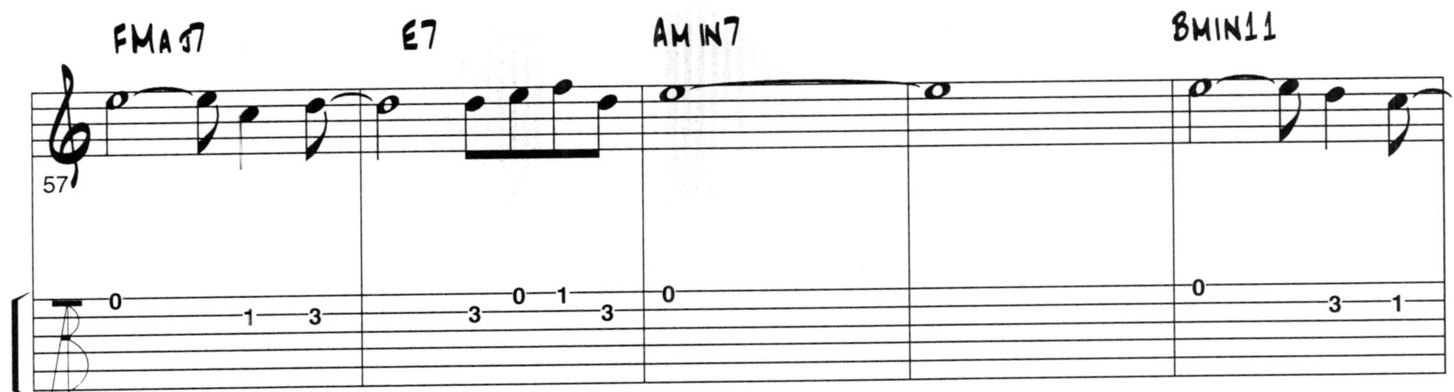
FMAJ7
E7
AMIN7
BMIN11
57

E7#5
AMIN7
GUITAR SOLO #1
62

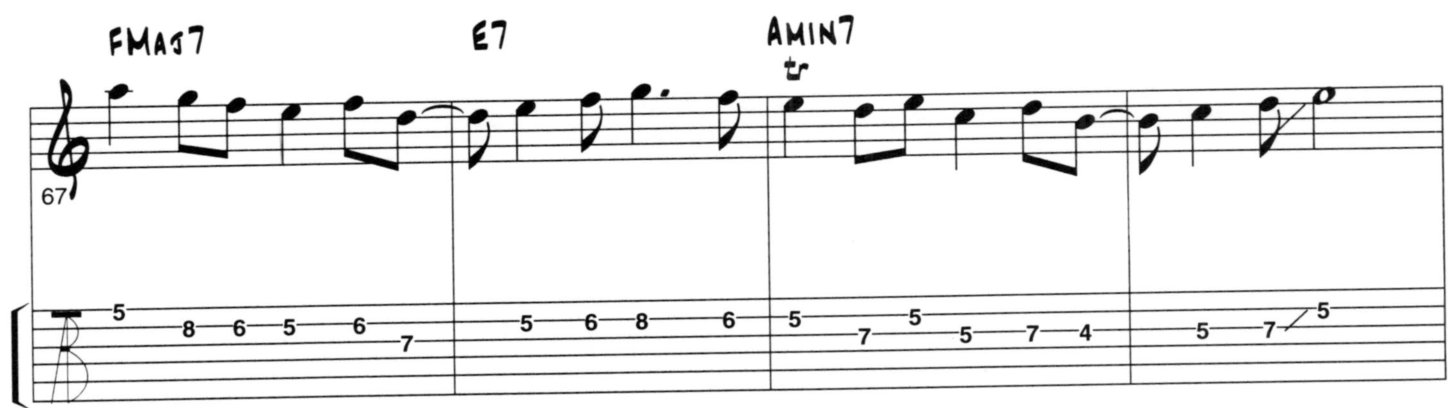
FMAJ7
E7
AMIN7
67

FMAJ7
E7♭9
AMIN7
71

FMAJ7
E7♭9
AMIN7
75

BMIN11
E7♯5
AMIN7
79

CODA (AFTER PIANO SOLO)
BMIN11
E7♯5
AMIN
83

BMIN11
E7♯5
87

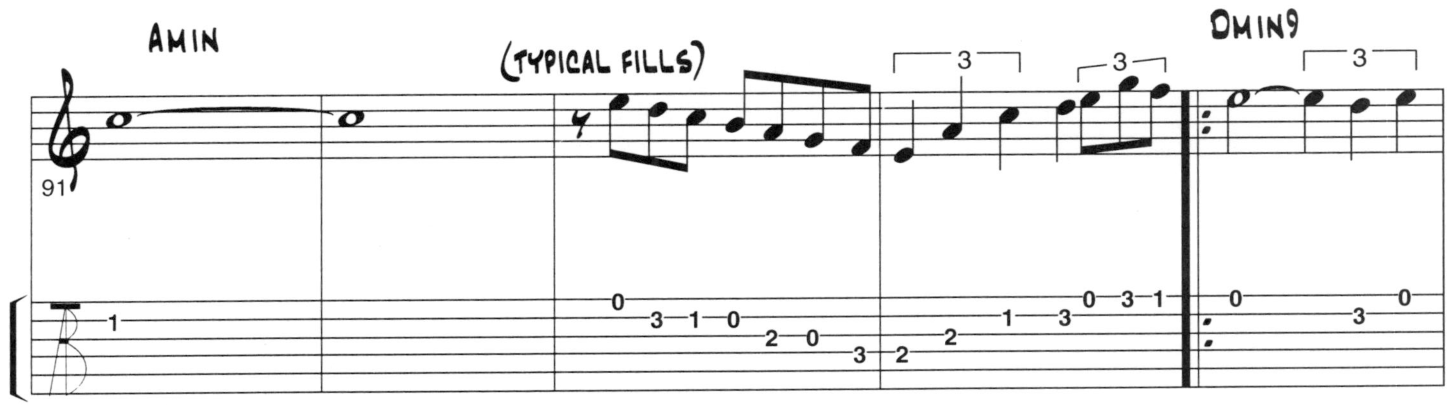
AMIN
(TYPICAL FILLS)
DMIN9
91

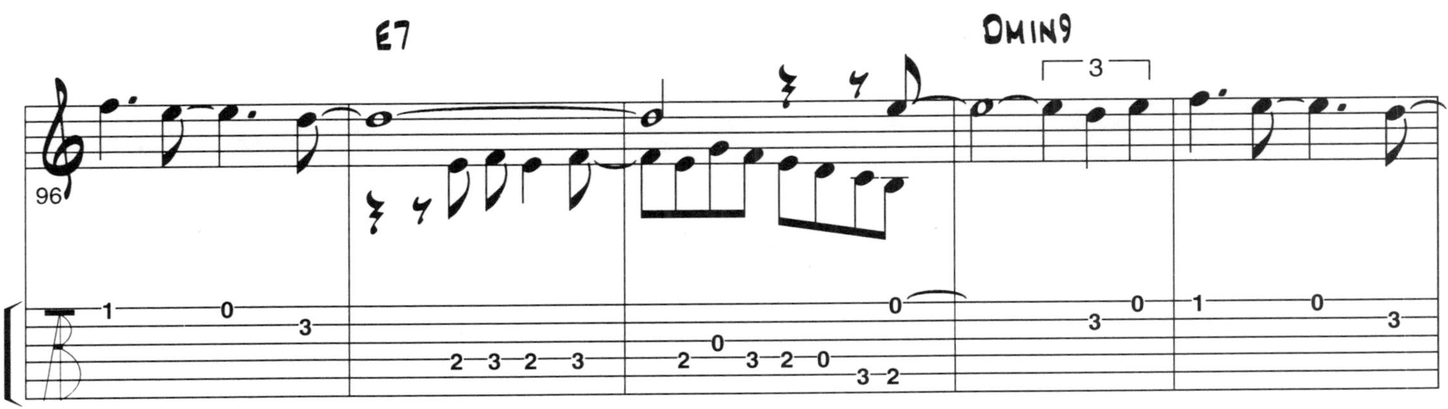
E7
DMIN9
96

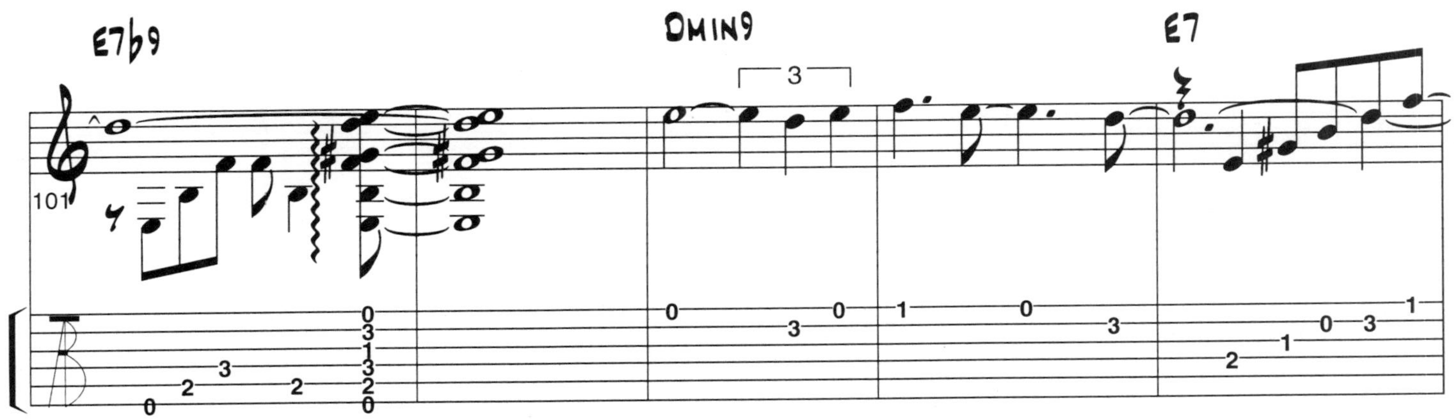
E7♭9
DMIN9
E7
101

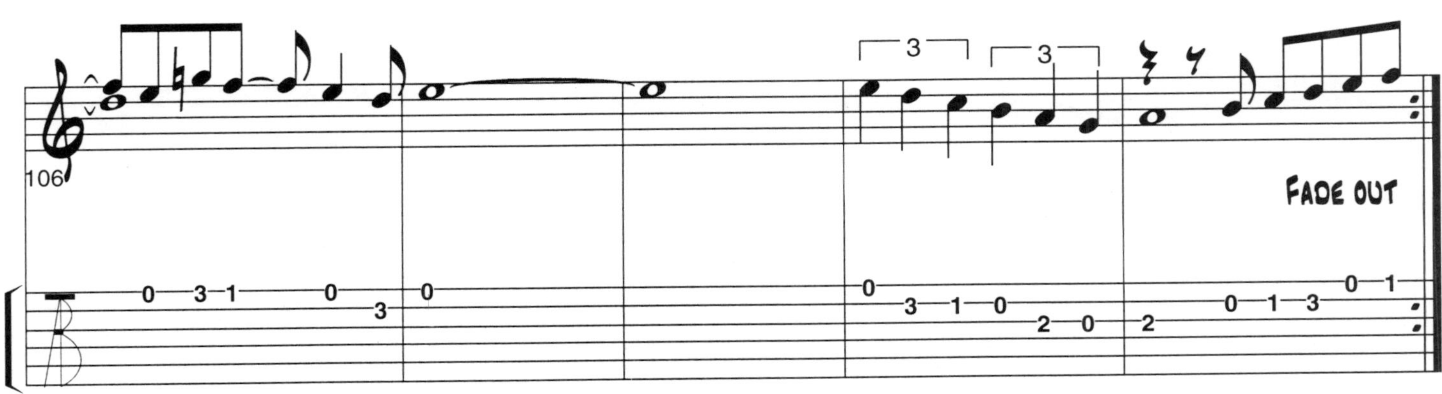
106
FADE OUT

PAQUETA, ISLE OF LOVE

B7
EMIN2
1
17
0 1 0 3 0 4 2
2
0
0 2 3 5

2
AMIN9
3
EMIN9
21
5 7 8 7 5
5 7 8 7 5
7 8 9

AMIN9
3
3
3
B7
25
5 7 8 7 5
5 7 8 7 5
7

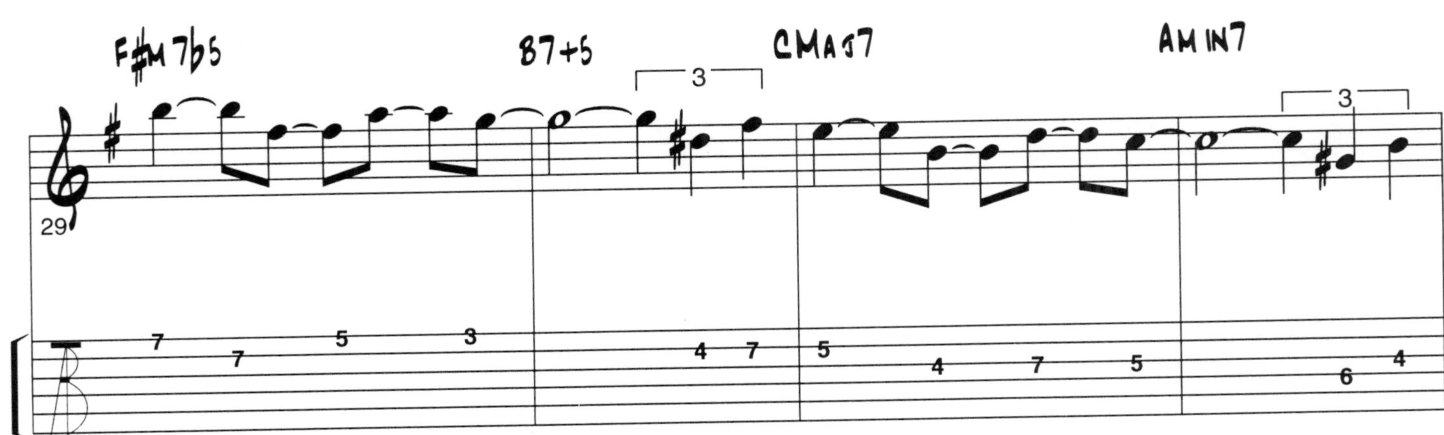
F#M7b5
B7+5
3
CMAJ7
AMIN7
3
29
7 7 5 3
4 7
5 4 7 5
6 4

B7
tr
EMIN2
EMIN
33
D.S. AL CODA
2
4 3 4 4 2
0

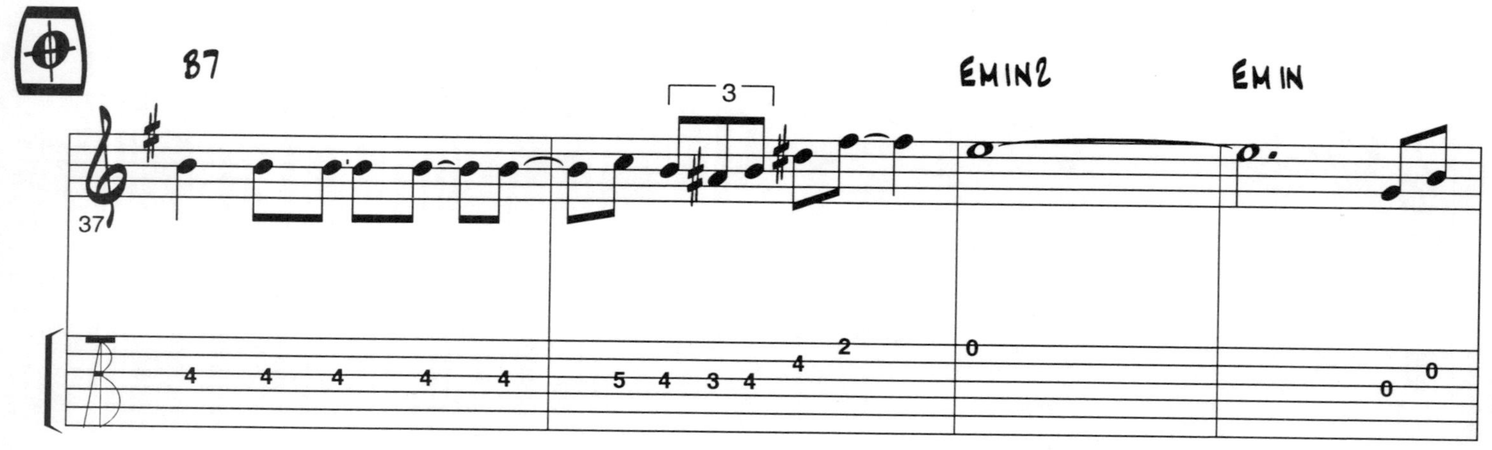
B7
3
EMIN2
EMIN
37
4 4 4 4 4
5 4 3 4 4 2
0
0 0

B7
EMIN2
EMIN
41
4 4
5 4 3 4 4 2
0

EMIN9
45
RIT.

Paqueta, Isle of Love (solo)

Jack Jezzro

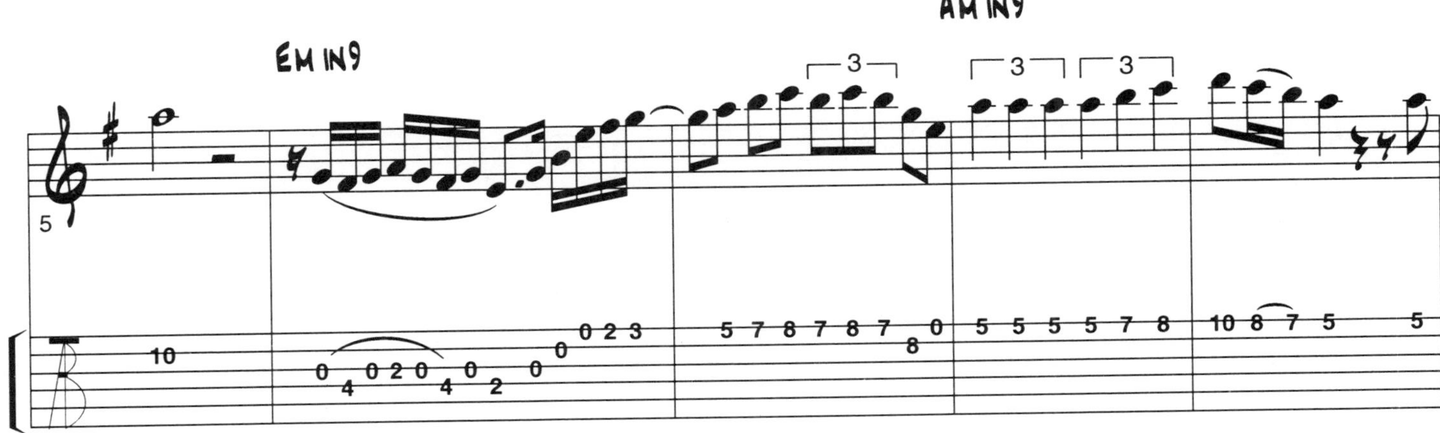

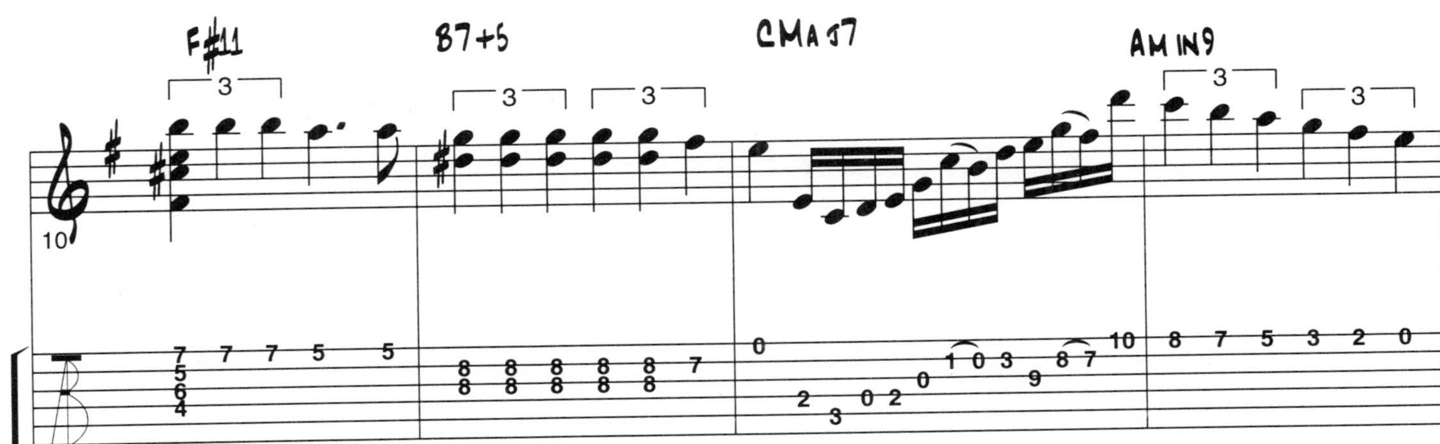

CAFE CALYPSO

JACK JEZZRO

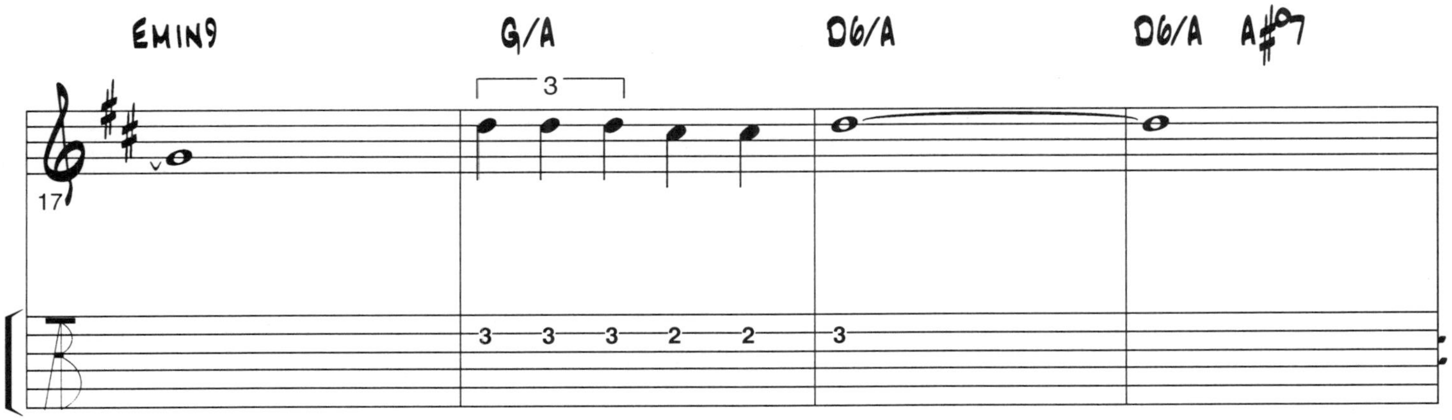
EMIN9
G/A
D6/A
D6/A A#°7
17

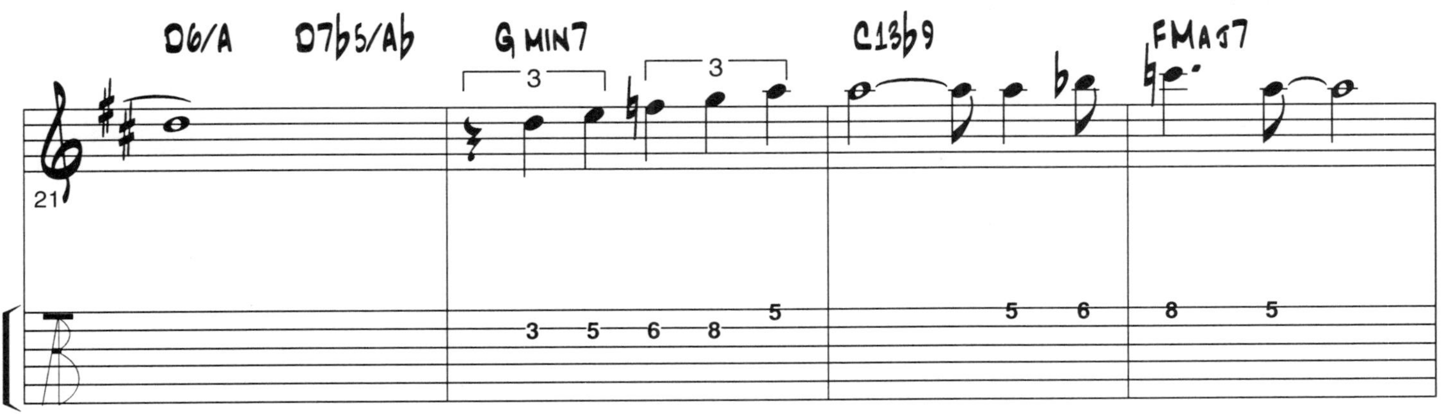
D6/A
D7b5/Ab
G MIN7
C13b9
FMAJ7
21

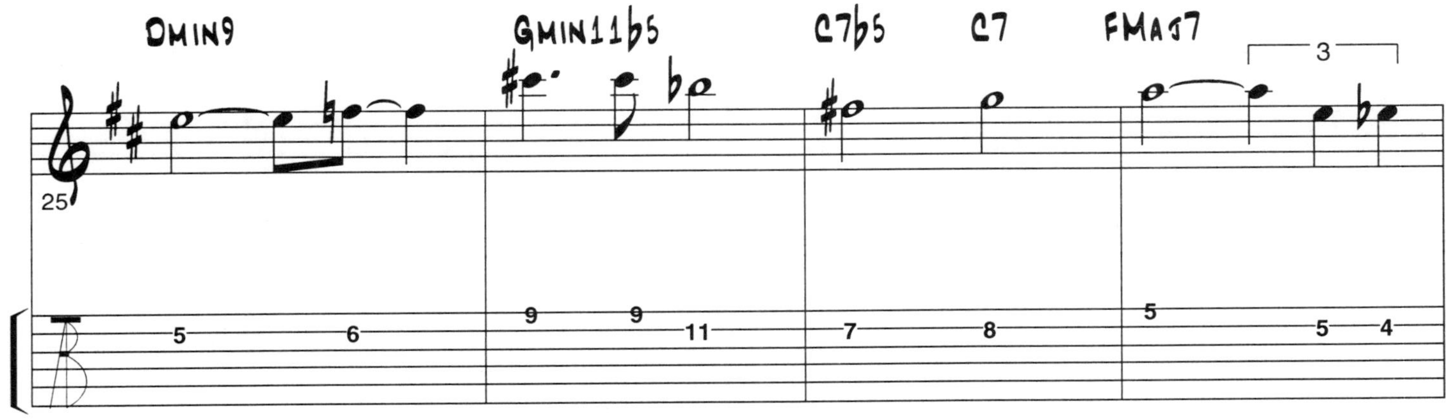
DMIN9
GMIN11b5
C7b5
C7
FMAJ7
25

F6
F MIN7
Bb13b9
EbMAJ7
29

CMIN9
F MIN7
B♭13
1
EMIN11♭5

2
A7+5
A#°7
EMIN9
A13
F#MIN11♭5
B7♭9
D.S. AL CODA

E MIN7
A13♭9

DMAJ9
GMIN6/D
(REPEAT WITH VARIATIONS AND FADE)

Cafe Calypso (solo)

(at 2:42, after pno solo) Jack Jezzro

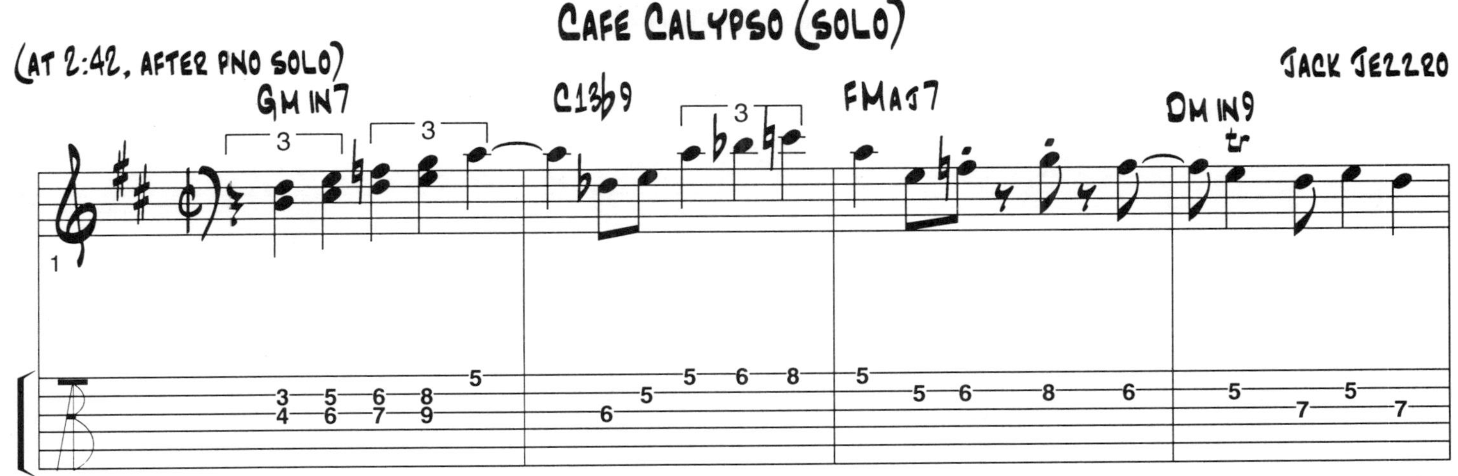

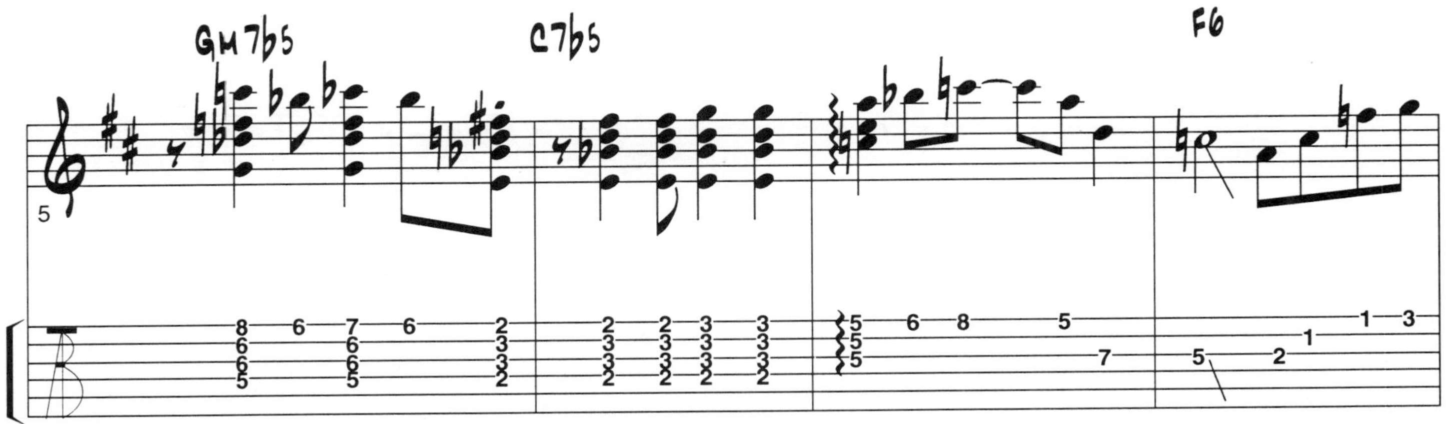

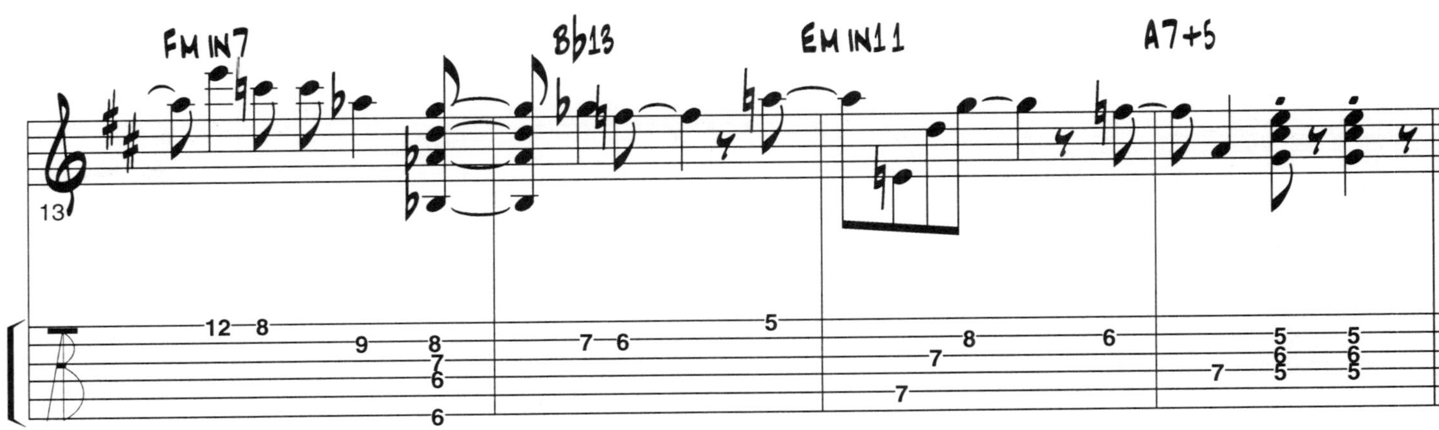

Latin Storm

Jack Jezzro

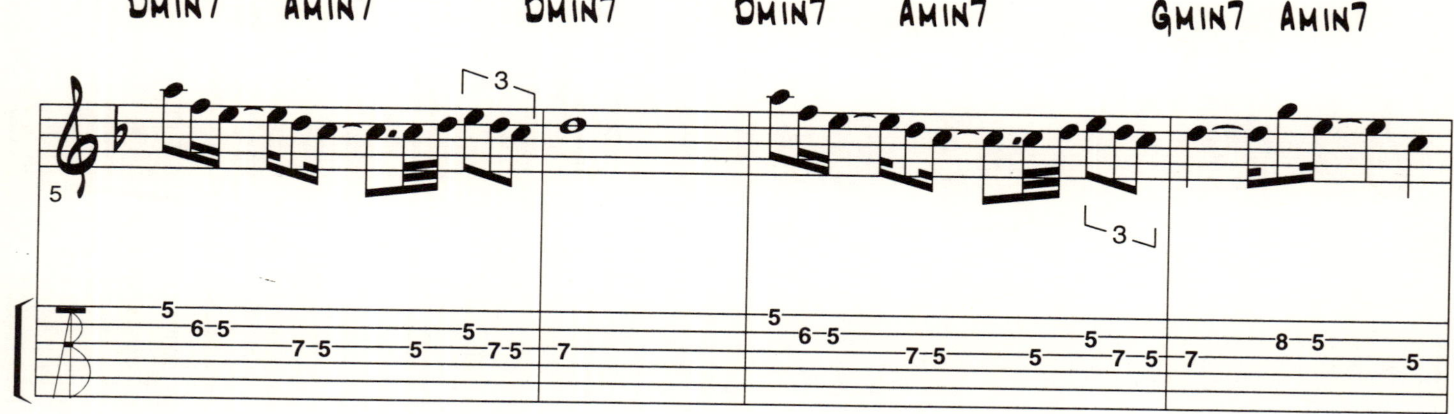

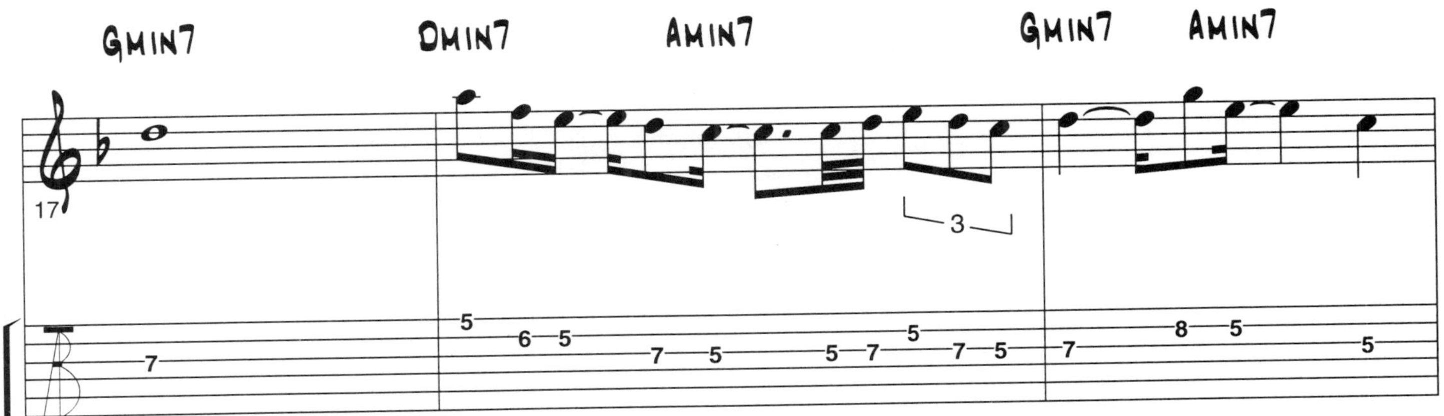
GMIN7
DMIN7
AMIN7
GMIN7
AMIN7
17

B♭MAJ7#11
AMIN11
GMIN7
AMIN7
DMIN7
20

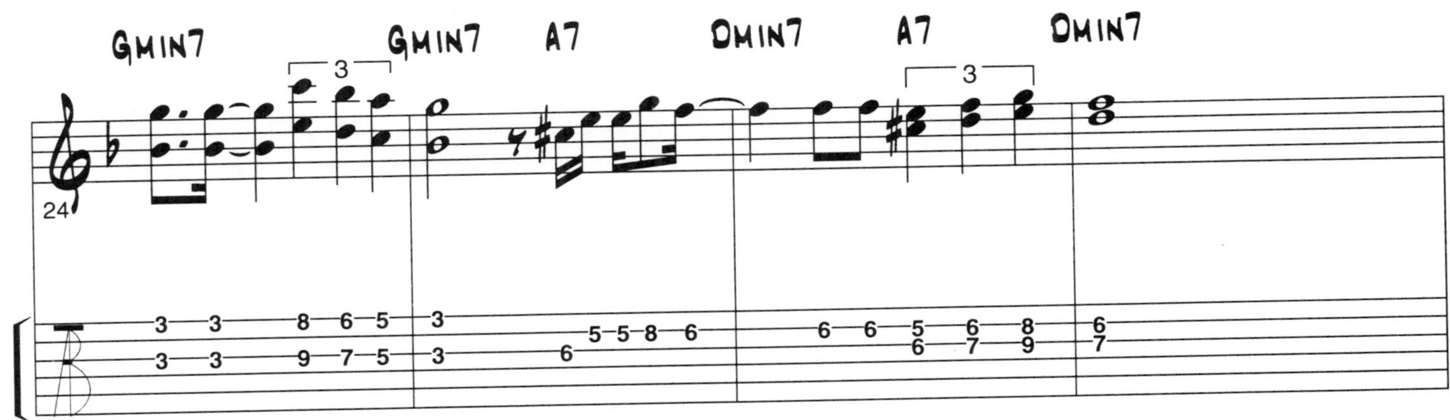
GMIN7
GMIN7
A7
DMIN7
A7
DMIN7
24

GMIN7
GMIN7
A7
DMIN7
B♭7
28

A7
DMIN7
AMIN11
GMIN7
31

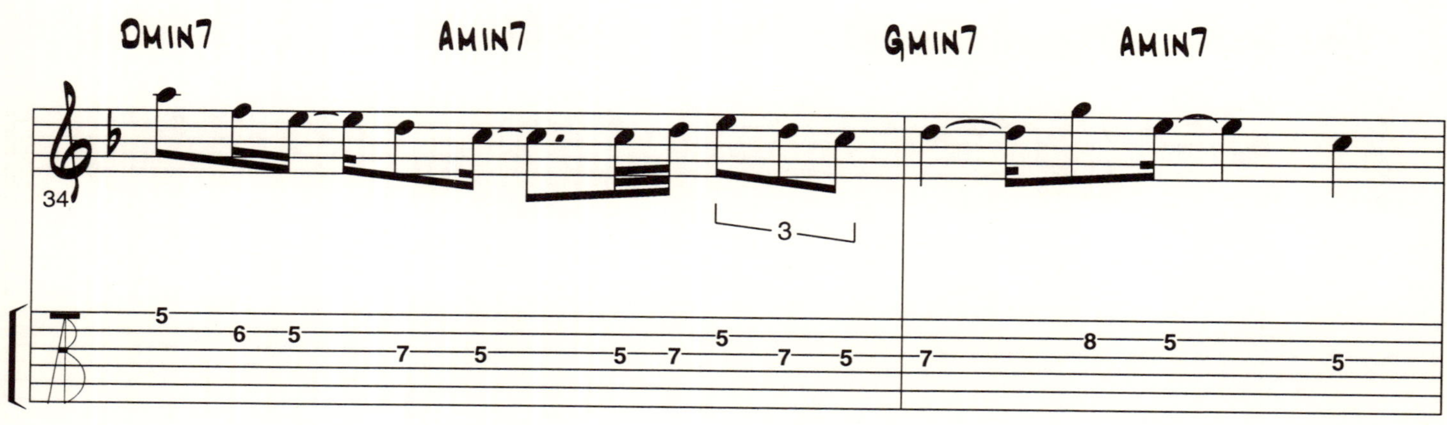
DMIN7
AMIN7
GMIN7
AMIN7
34

B♭MAJ7#11
AMIN11
DMIN7
GMIN7/D
36

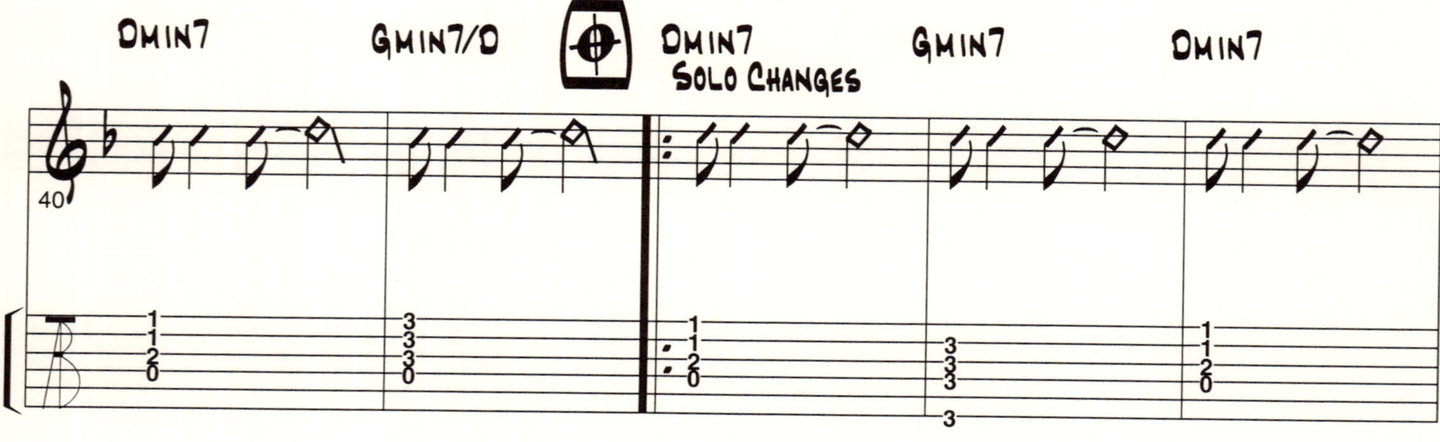
DMIN7
GMIN7/D
DMIN7
SOLO CHANGES
GMIN7
DMIN7
40

A7
B♭MAJ7#11
GMIN7
B♭MAJ7#11
45
1
A7
2
A7
DMIN7
GMIN7
49
A7
DMIN7
A7
DMIN7
GMIN7
B♭7
53
A7
B♭7
1
A7
2
GMIN7
A7
57

DMIN7
GMIN7
GMIN7
A7
DMIN7
A7
61

DMIN7
GMIN7
GMIN7
A7
65

DMIN7
B♭7
A7
68
D.S. AL CODA

DMIN7
GMIN7/D
DMIN7
GMIN7/D
70
FADE OUT

This page has been left blank to avoid awkward page turns.

Latin Storm (solo)

(at 1:26; note change of time signature)

Jack Jezzro

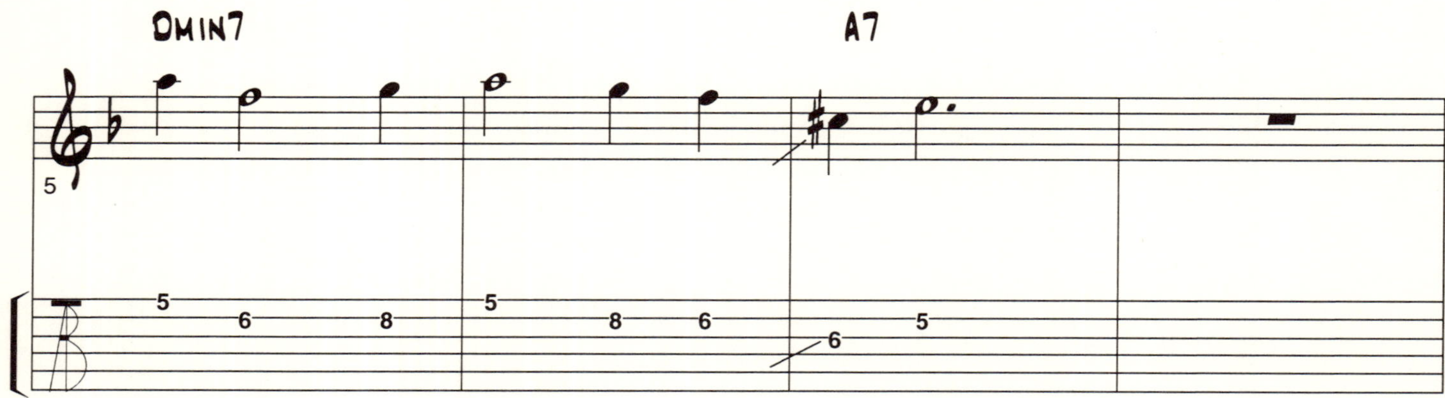

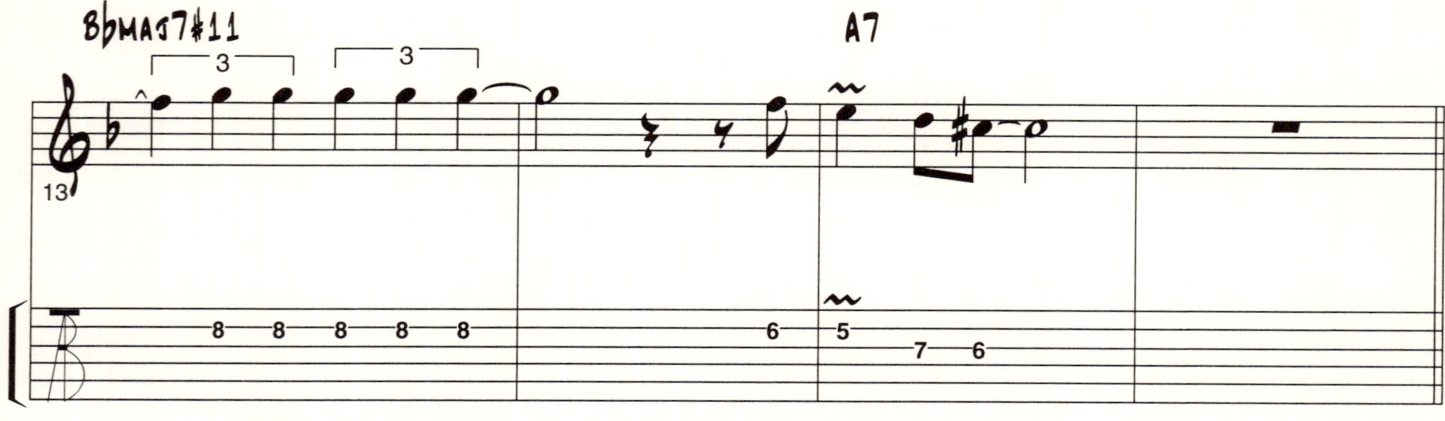

DMIN7
GMIN7
17

DMIN7
A7
21

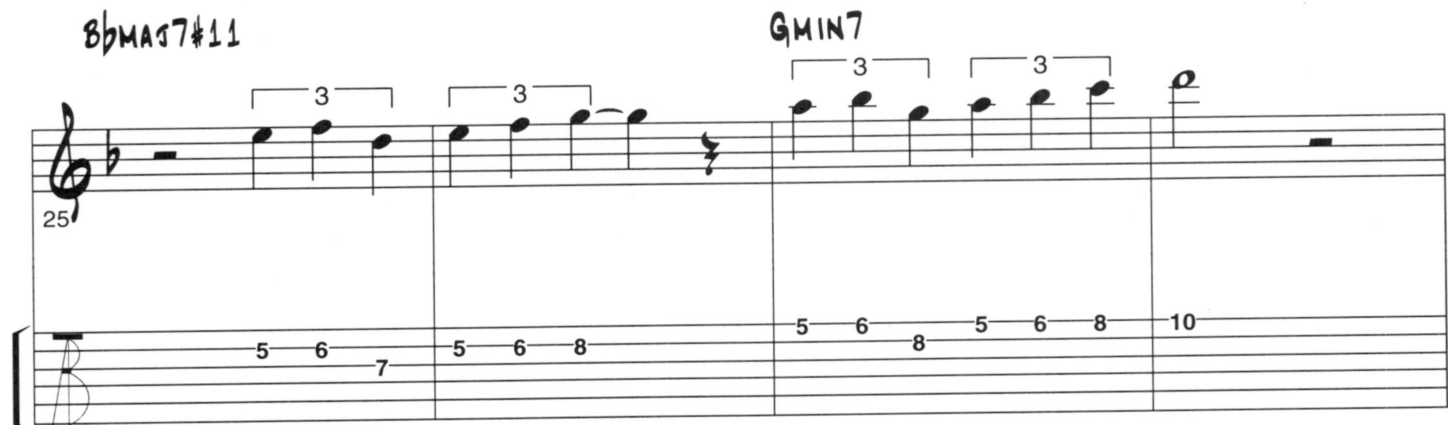
B♭MAJ7#11
GMIN7
25

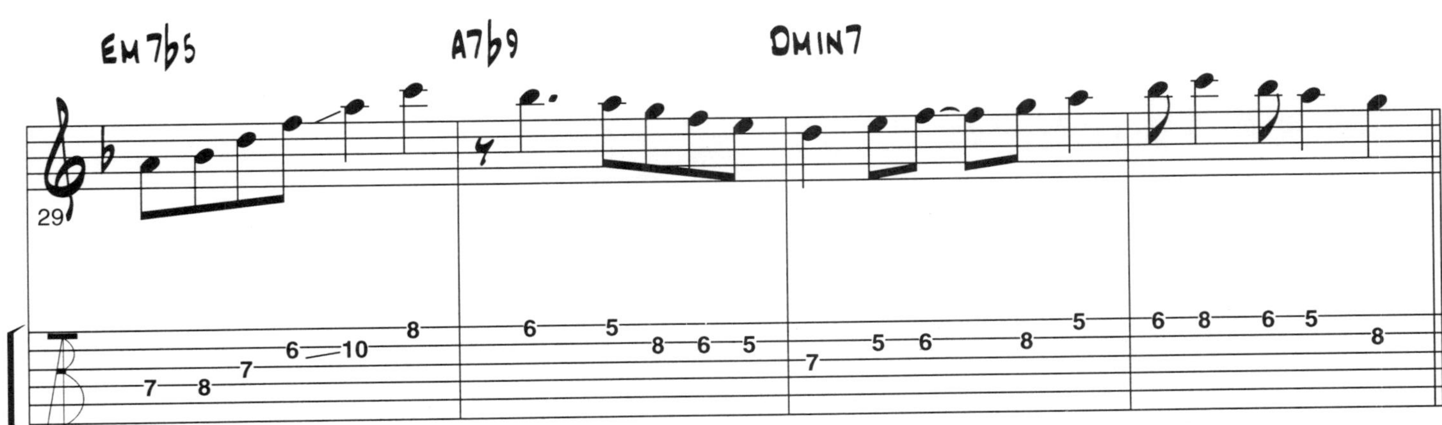
EM7♭5
A7♭9
DMIN7
29

Miranda
Jack Jezzro
CMaj7
Amin7
B7
Emin
Rhythm pattern behind trumpet intro
Amin7
B7
Emin2
(Continue with variations through repeat)
Emin
Emin9/D
CMaj7
B7
Emin2
Amin7
Emin2

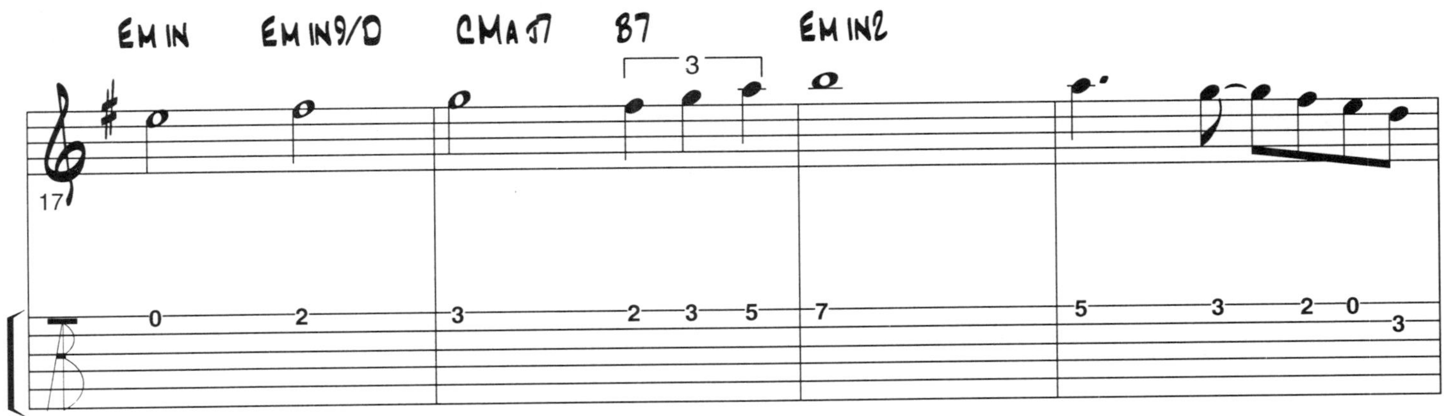
EMIN
EMIN9/D
CMAJ7
B7
EMIN2
17

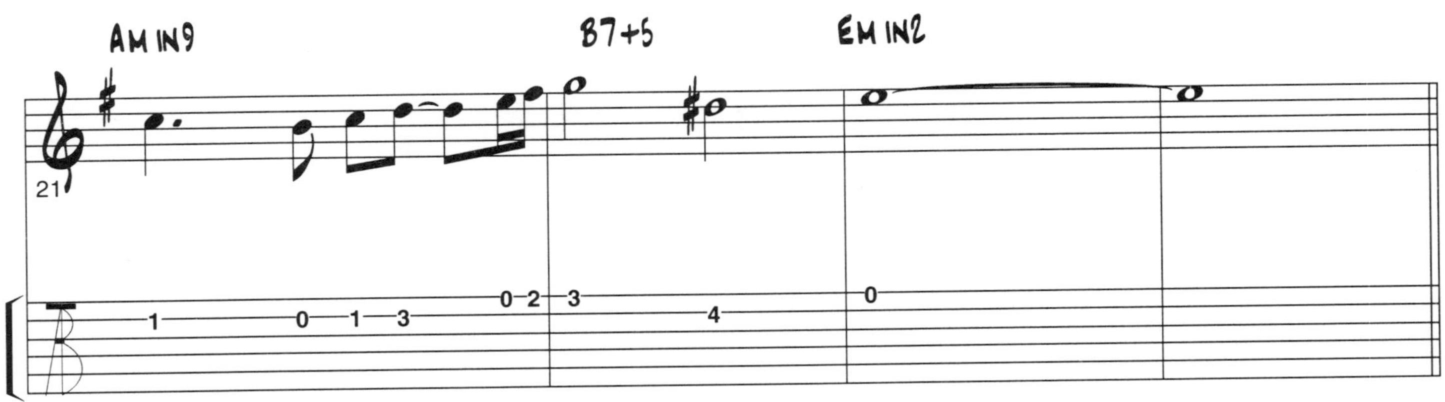
AMIN9
B7+5
EMIN2
21

D
AMIN7
EMIN7
25

D
AMIN7
C2
29

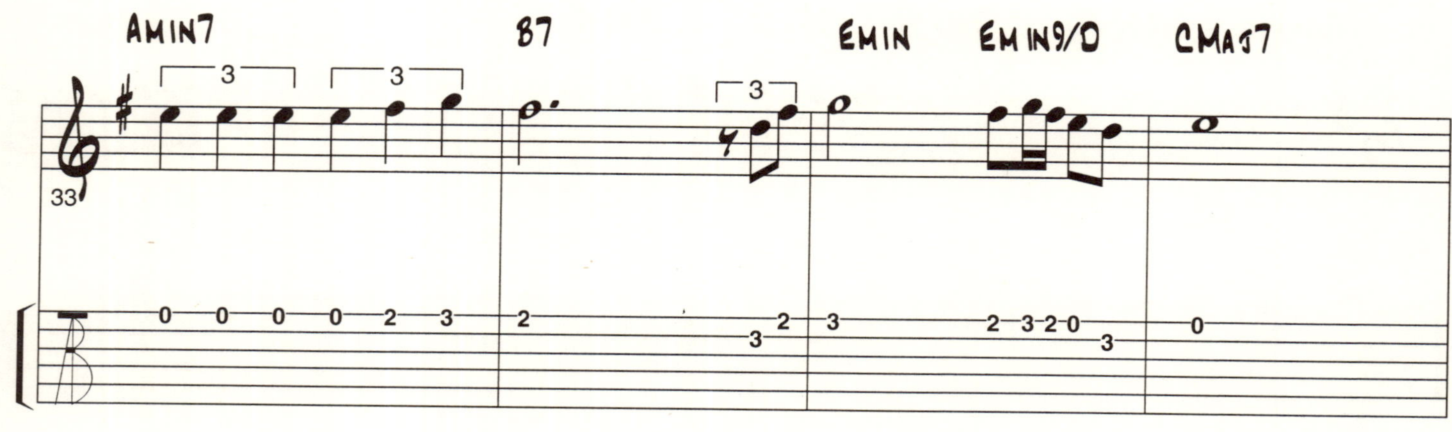
AMIN7
B7
EMIN
EMIN9/D
CMAJ7
33

AMIN9
B7+5
EMIN9
EMIN
(PICKUP TO SOLO)
37

GUITAR SOLO (AT 1:39)
AMIN
EMIN
41

AMIN
B7+5
44

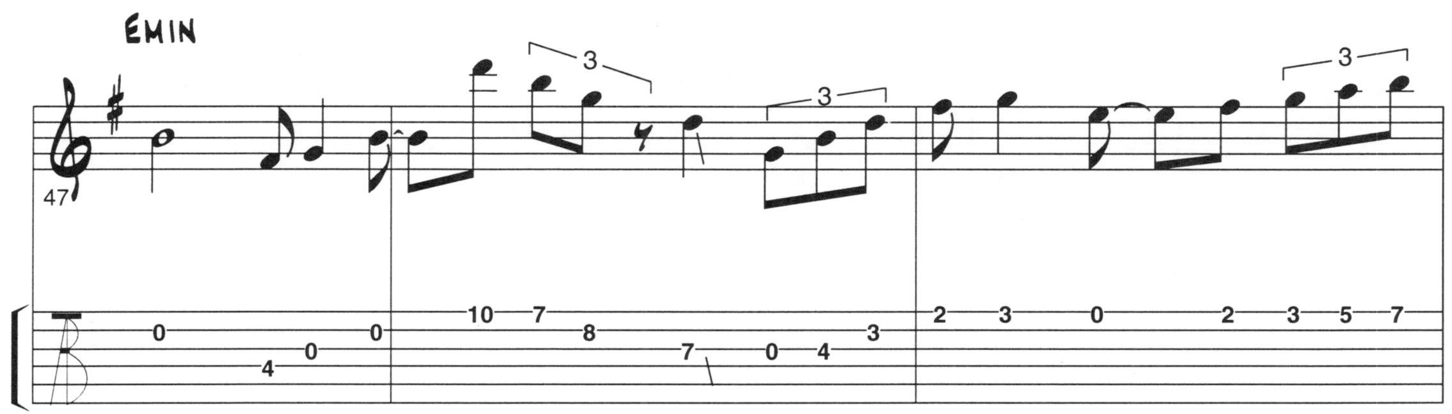
EMIN

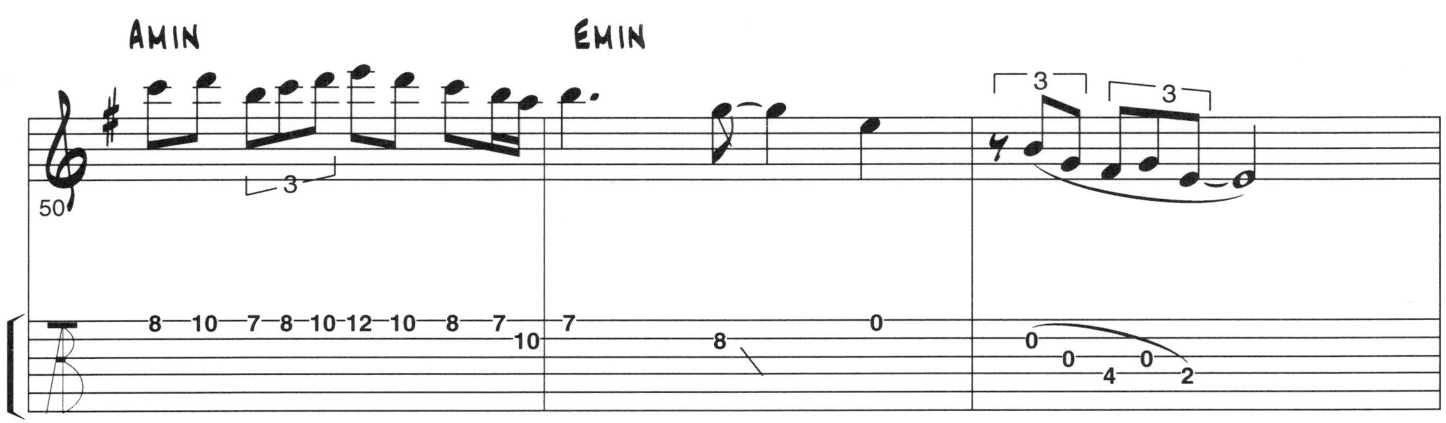
AMIN
EMIN

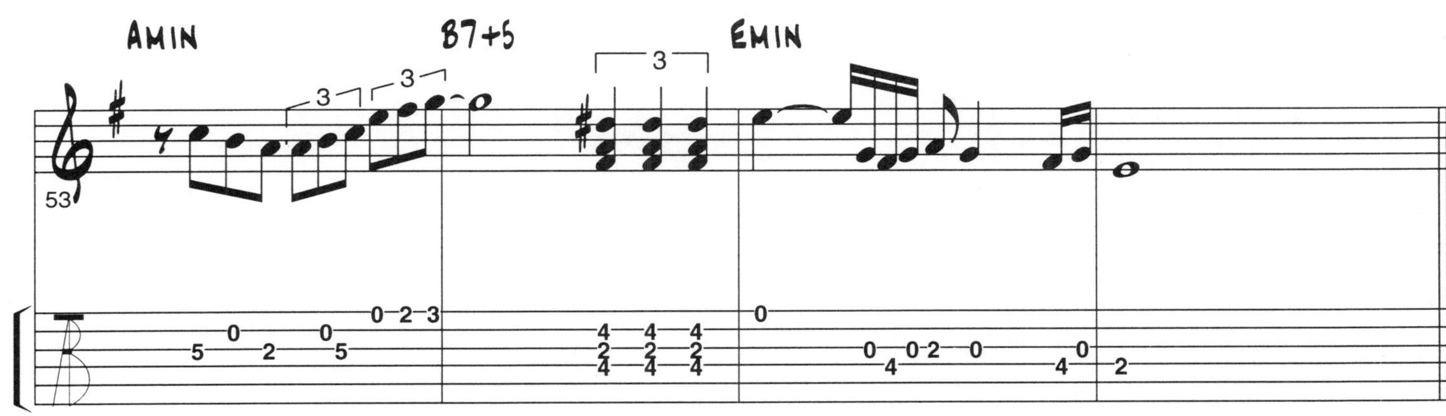
AMIN
B7+5
EMIN

CMAJ7
AMIN7
B7
EMIN
TRUMPET INTERLUDE (SAME FIGURES AS INTRO)

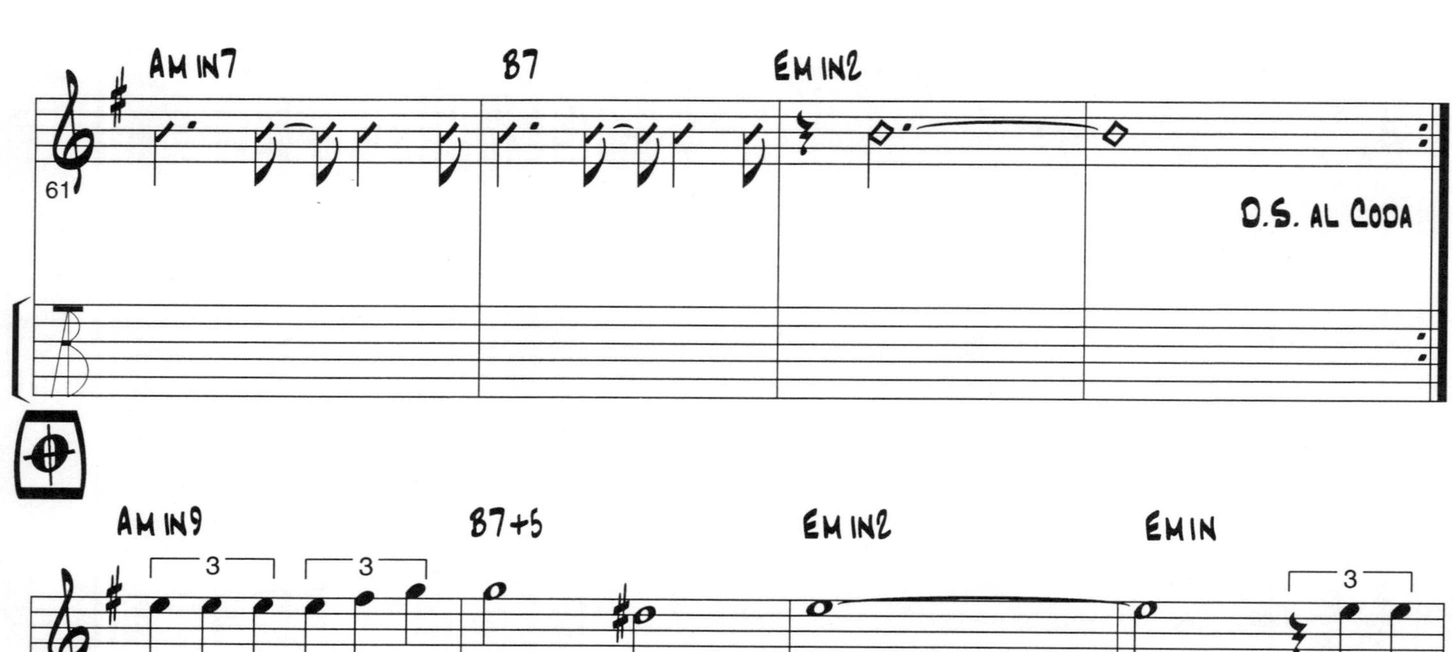

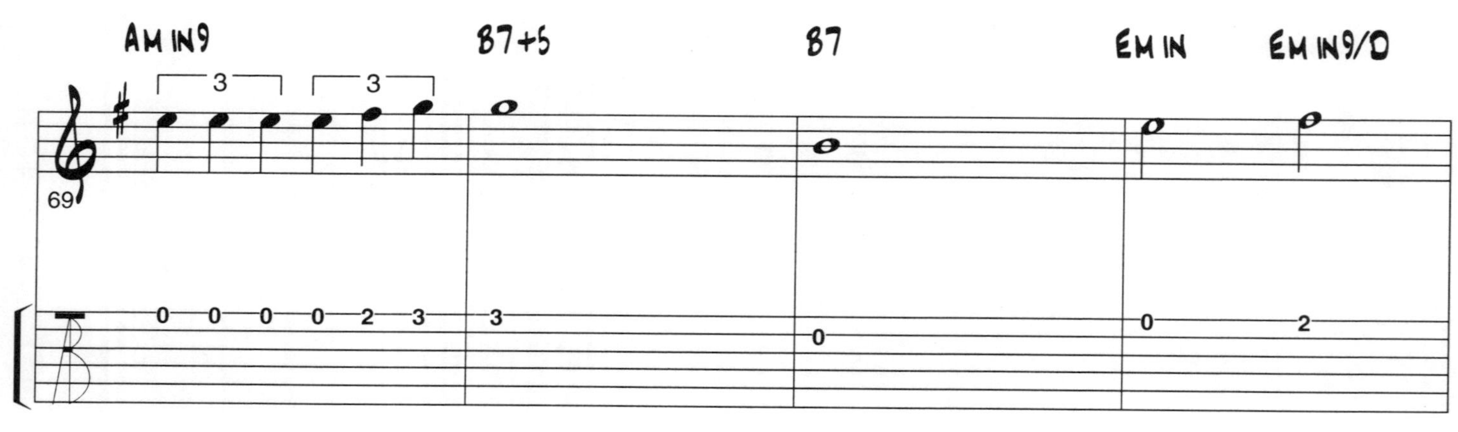

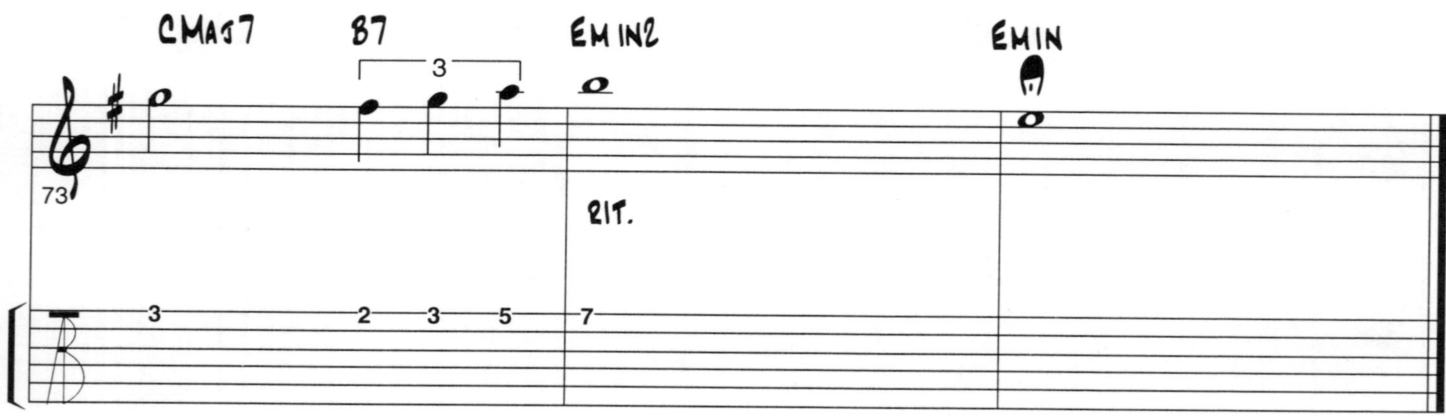

CMAJ7 B7 EMIN2 EMIN

73

RIT.

The Road to Ponta Pora

Jack Jezzro

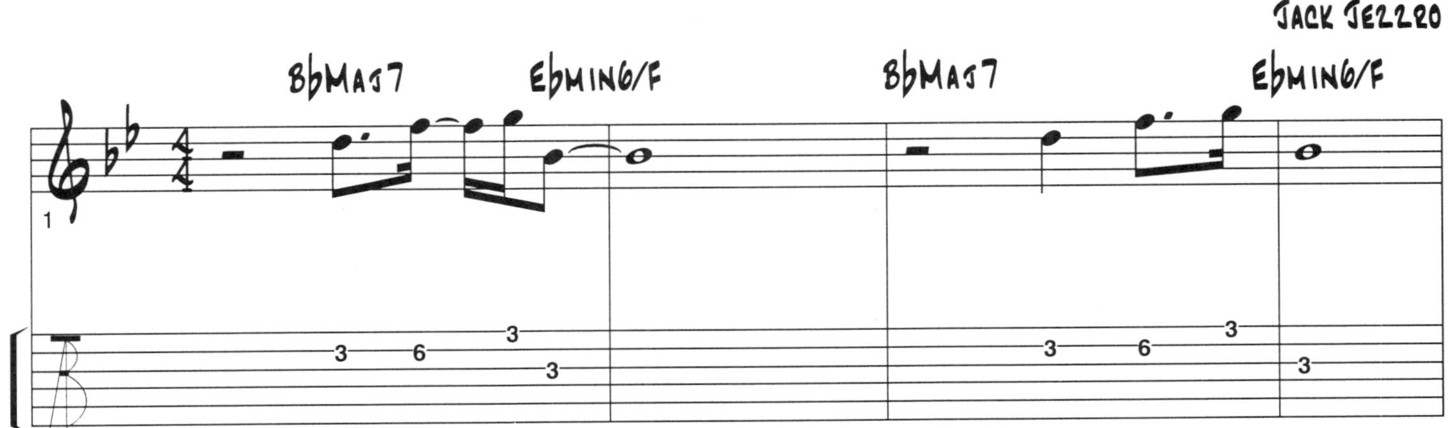
BbMaj7
EbMin6/F
BbMaj7
EbMin6/F

BbMaj7
CMin7/F
BbMaj7
EbMin6/F

BbMaj7
CMin7/F
BbMaj7

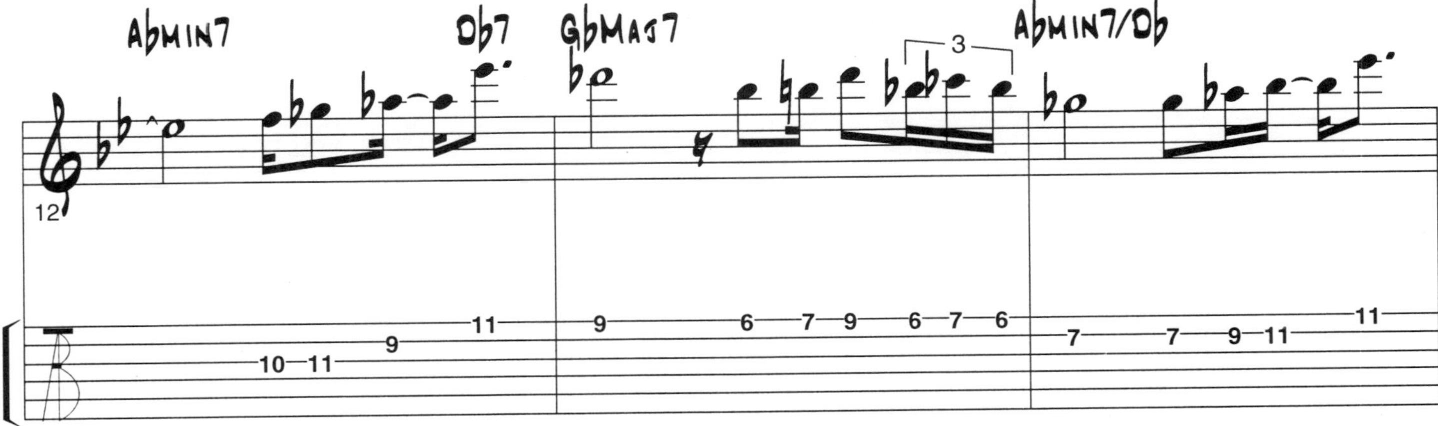
AbMin7
Db7
GbMaj7
AbMin7/Db

G♭MAJ7
EMIN7
A7SUS
DMAJ7
15

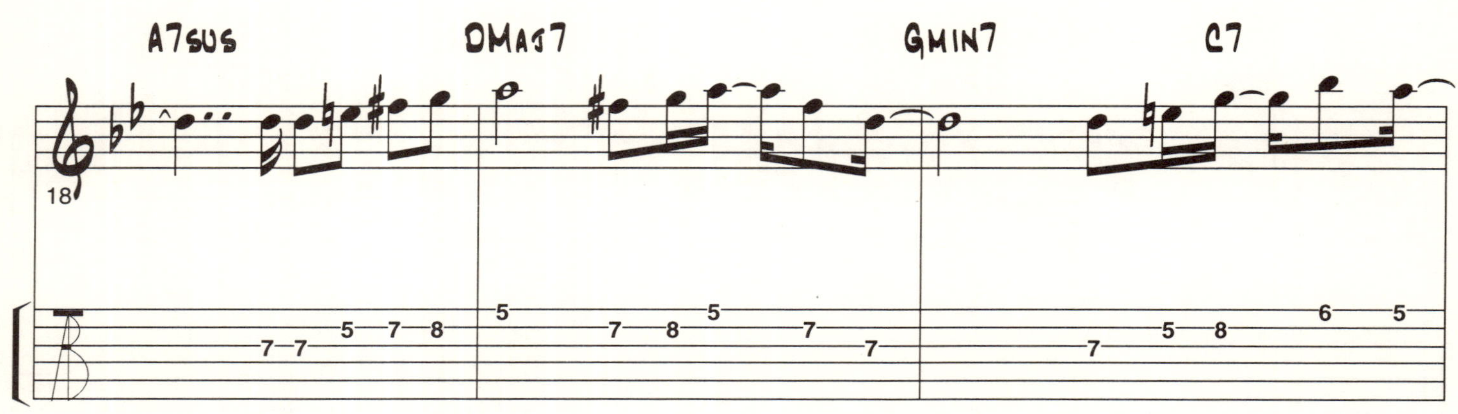
A7SUS
DMAJ7
GMIN7
C7
18

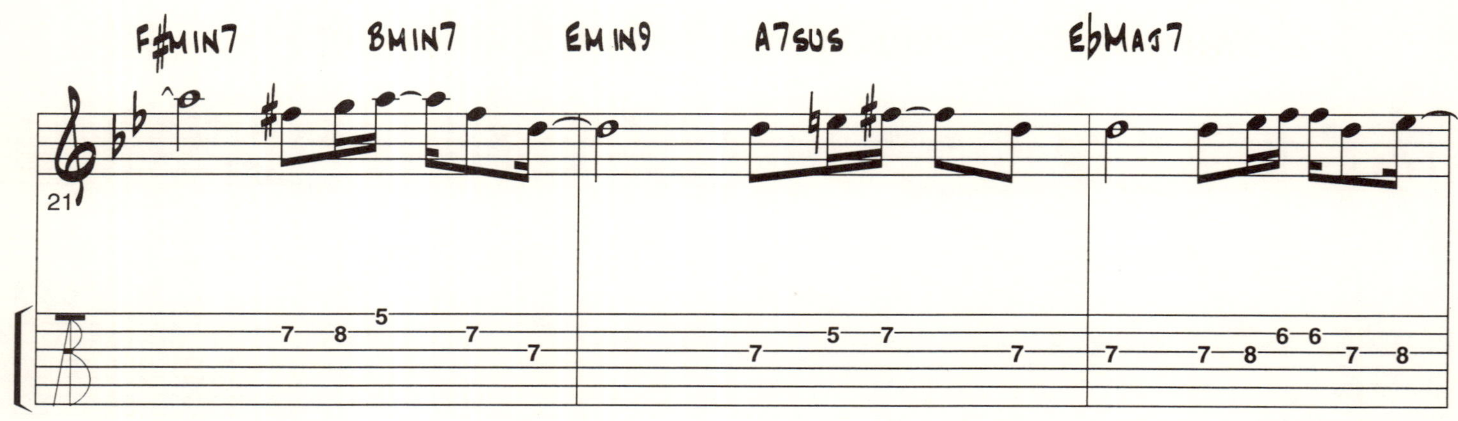
F♯MIN7
BMIN7
EMIN9
A7SUS
E♭MAJ7
21

D♭MAJ9
E♭MAJ9
CMIN7
CMIN7/F
24

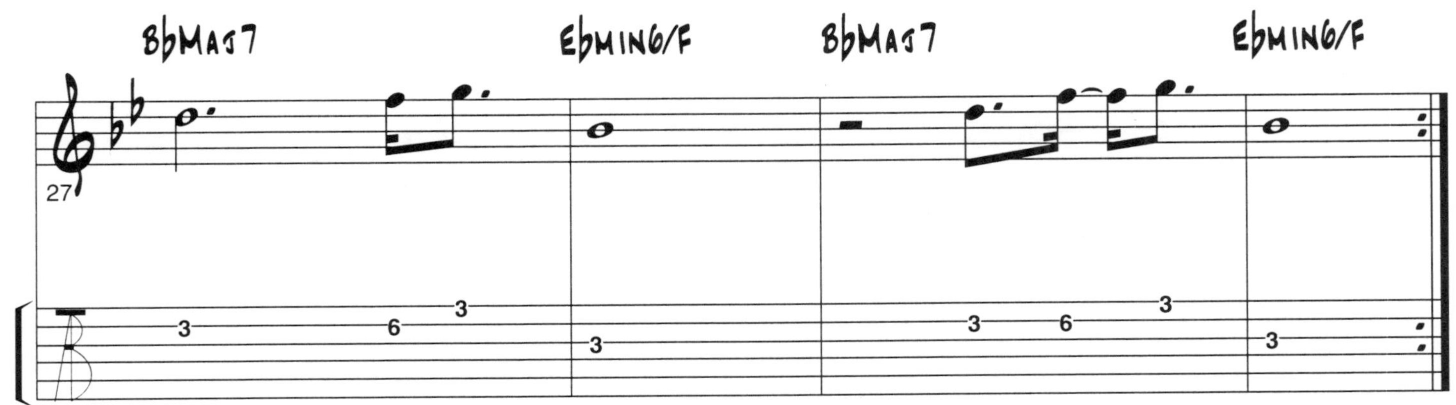
B♭MAJ7
E♭MIN6/F
B♭MAJ7
E♭MIN6/F
27

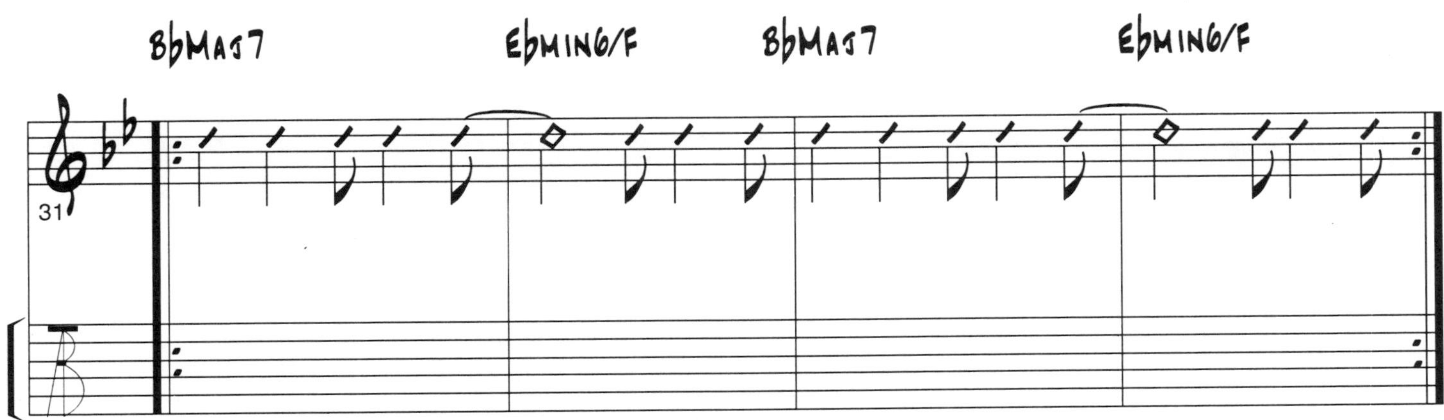
B♭MAJ7
E♭MIN6/F
B♭MAJ7
E♭MIN6/F
31

The Road to Ponta Pora (Solo)

13

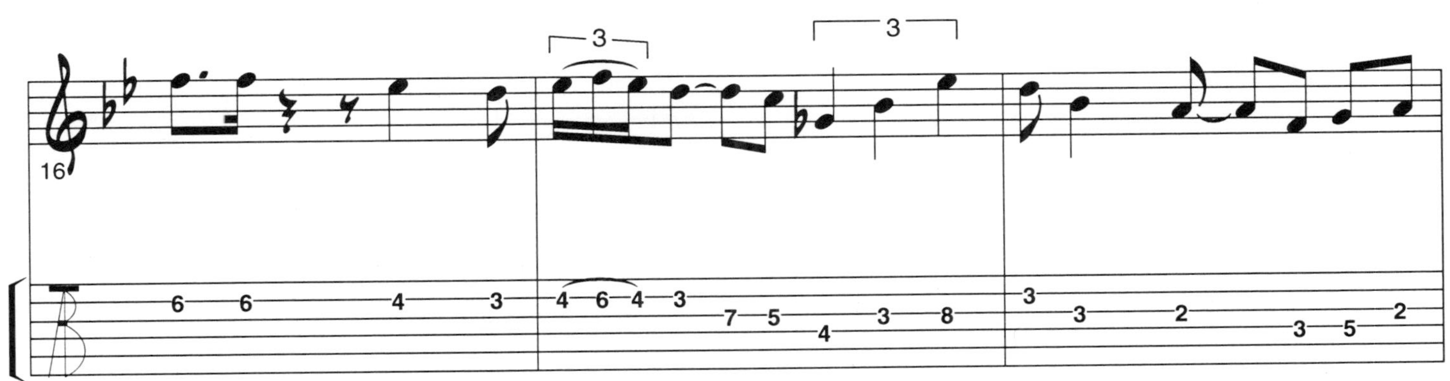
16

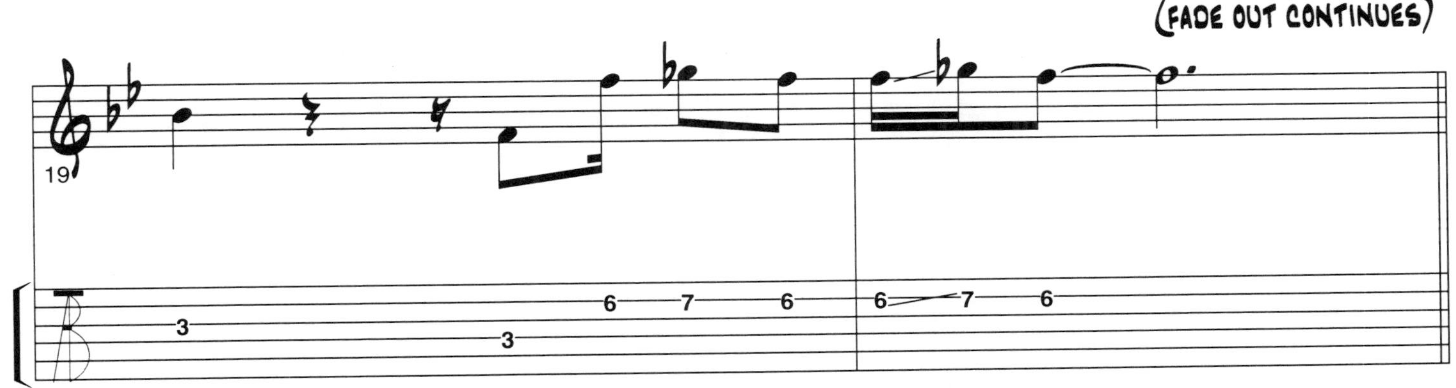
(FADE OUT CONTINUES)
19

Ladron de Corazon

Chris McDonald

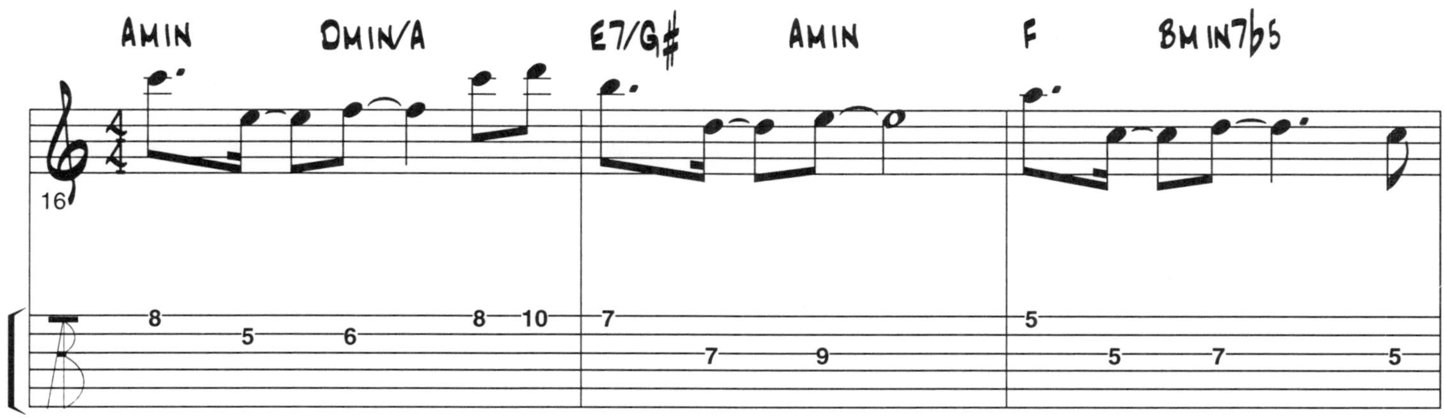
AMIN
DMIN/A
E7/G#
AMIN
F
BMIN7b5
16

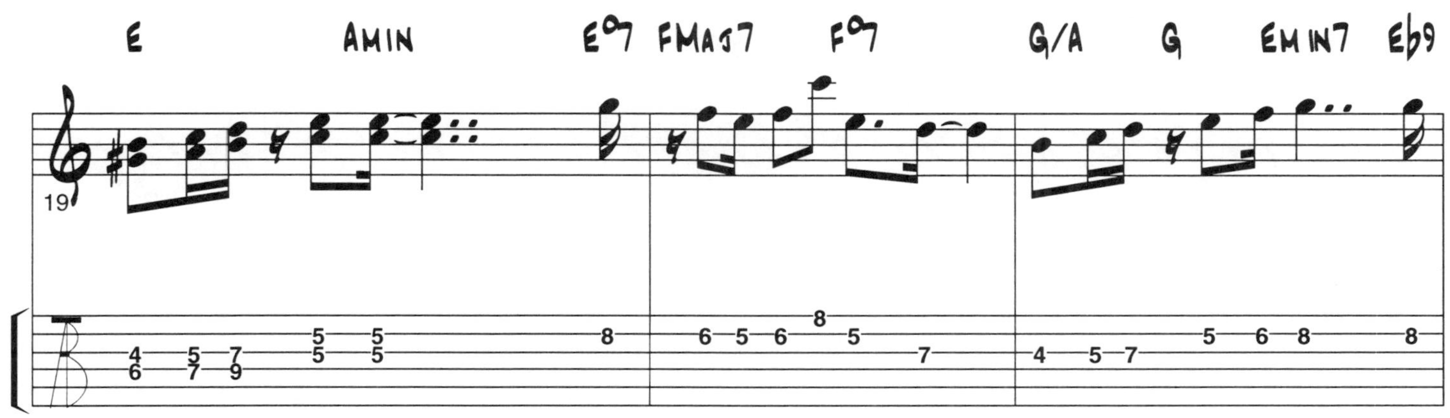
E
AMIN
E°7
FMAJ7
F°7
G/A
G
EMIN7
Eb9
19

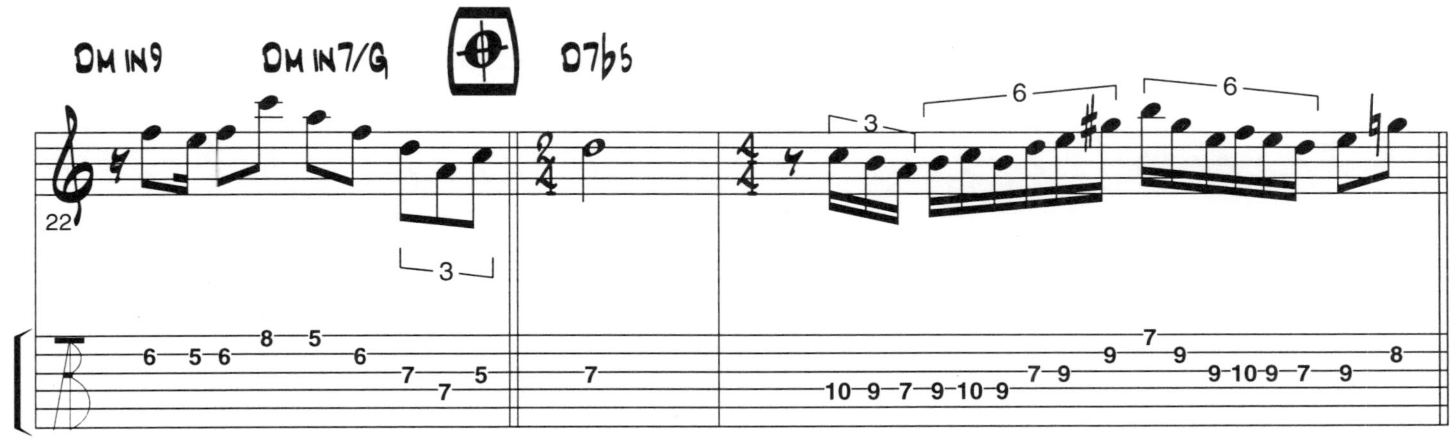
DMIN9
DMIN7/G
D7b5
22

AMIN
FMAJ7
C
E/G#
25

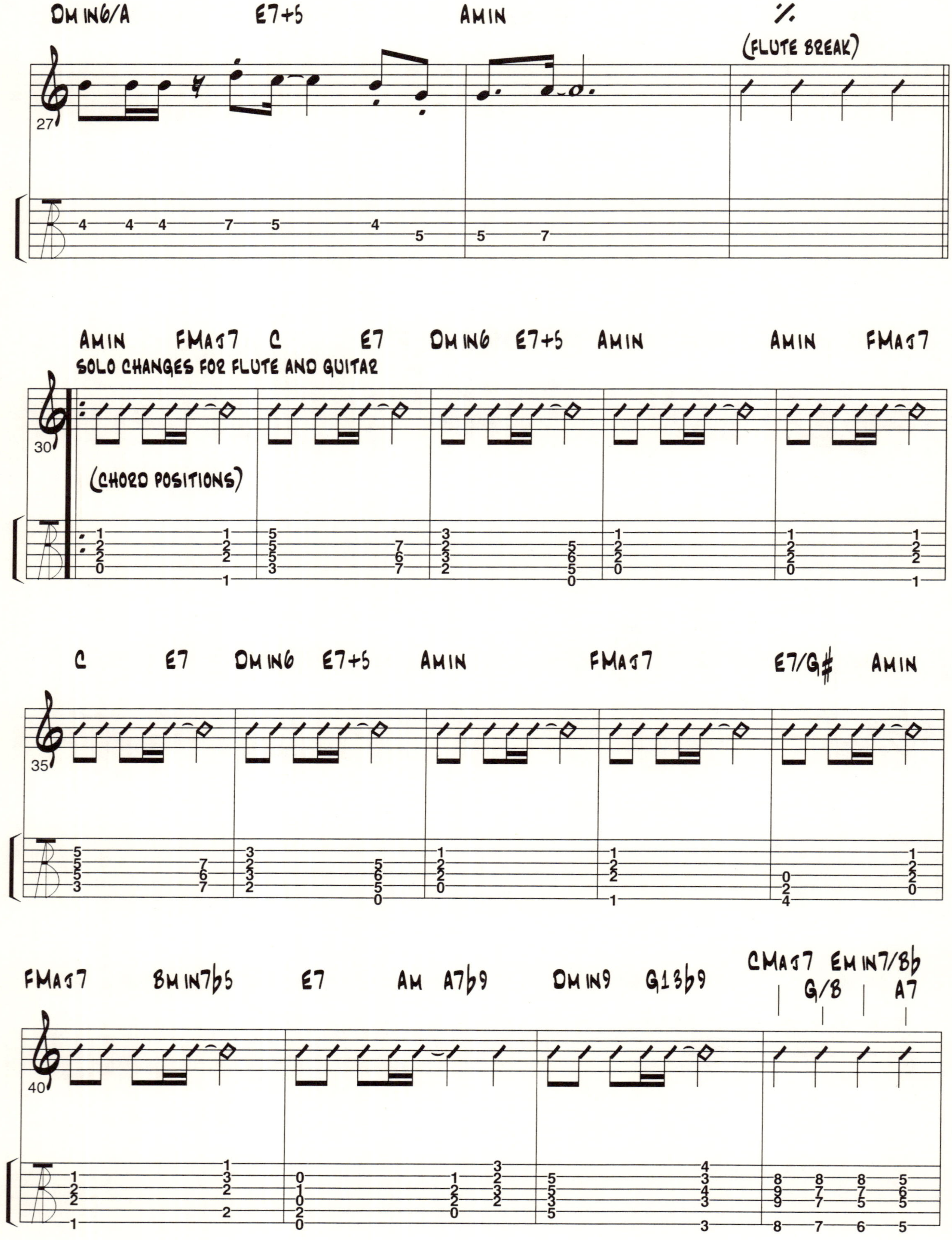

DMIN6/A
E7+5
AMIN
%
(FLUTE BREAK)
AMIN
FMAJ7
C
E7
DMIN6
E7+5
AMIN
AMIN
FMAJ7
SOLO CHANGES FOR FLUTE AND GUITAR
(CHORD POSITIONS)
C
E7
DMIN6
E7+5
AMIN
FMAJ7
E7/G#
AMIN
FMAJ7
BMIN7b5
E7
AM
A7b9
DMIN9
G13b9
CMAJ7
G/B
EMIN7/Bb
A7

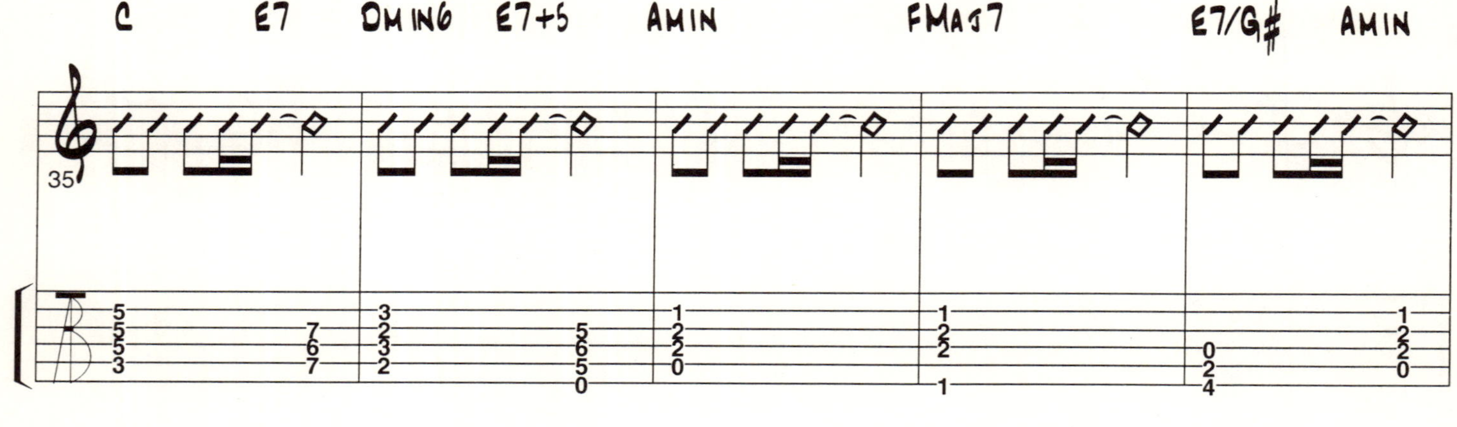

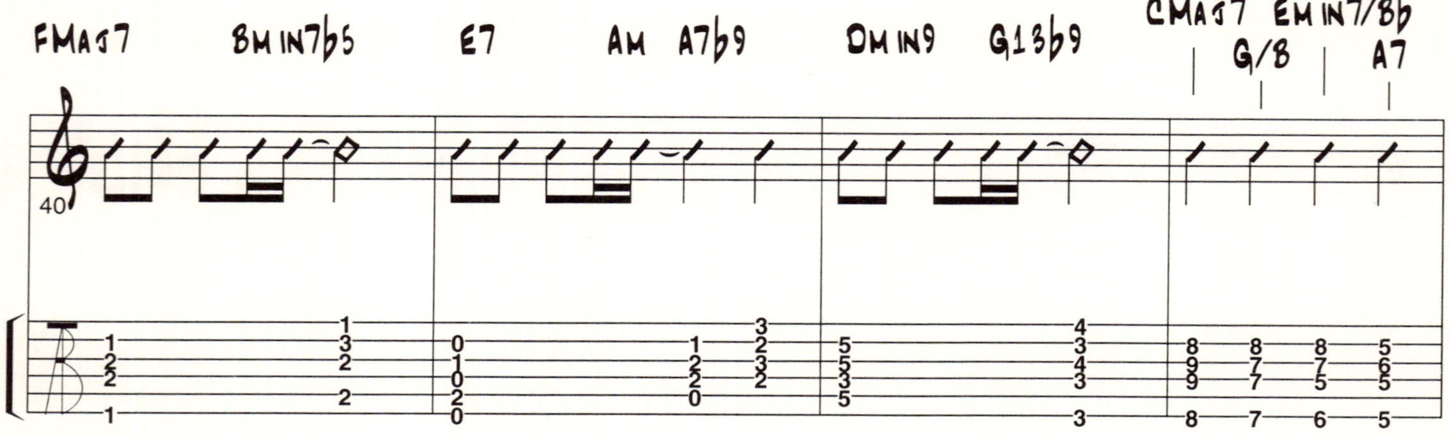

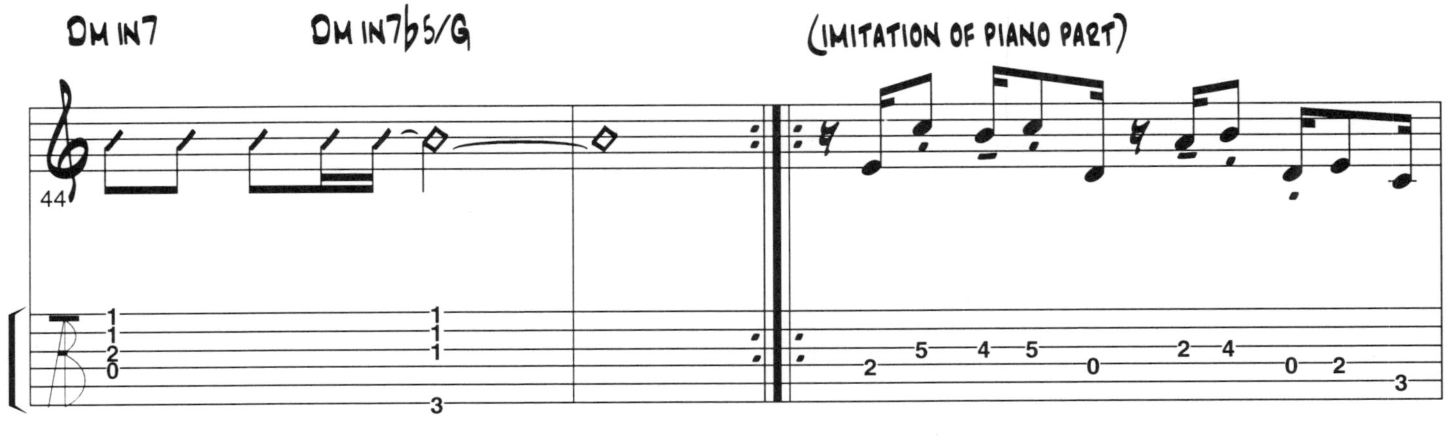
DMIN7
DMIN7♭5/G
(IMITATION OF PIANO PART)

AMIN11
AMIN11
D.S. AL CODA (W/REPEAT)

The Beach at Ipanema

Jack Jezzro

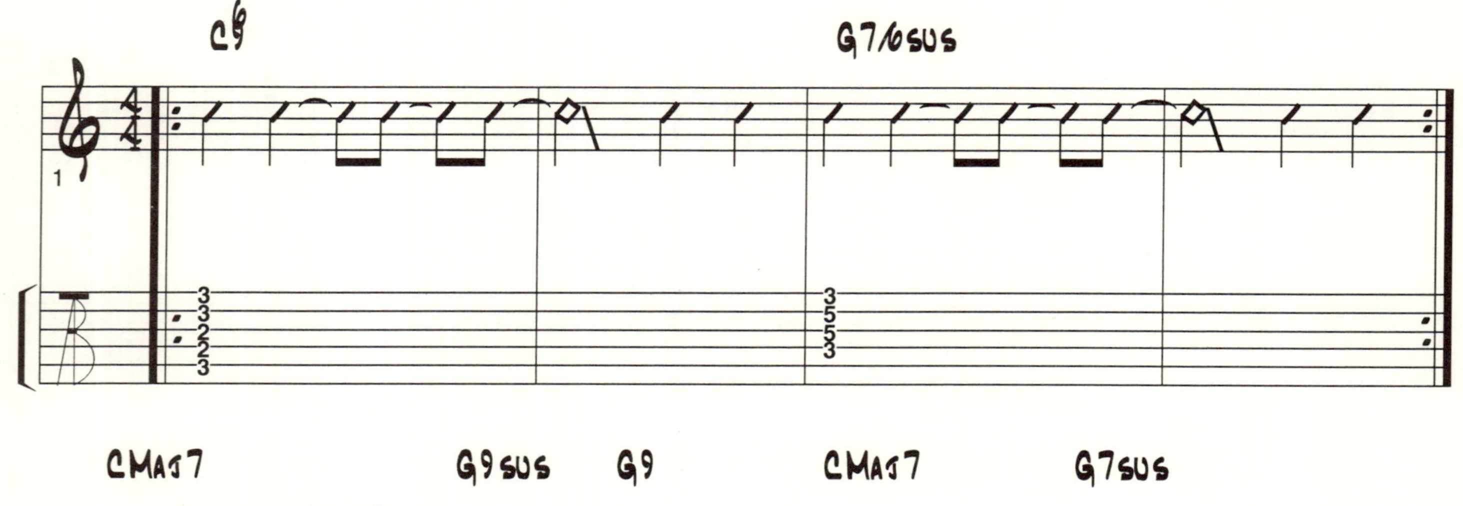

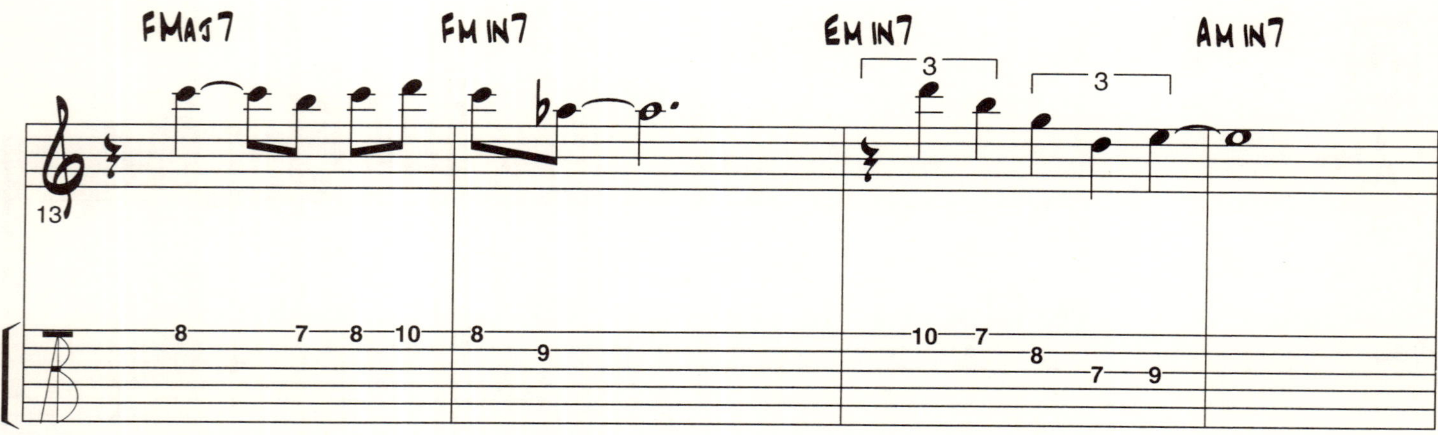

DMIN7
A7+5
D7♭5/A♭
1
G13 ♭9
17

2
DMIN7
D7♭5/A♭
G13 ♭9
C6
C7♭5/G♭
21

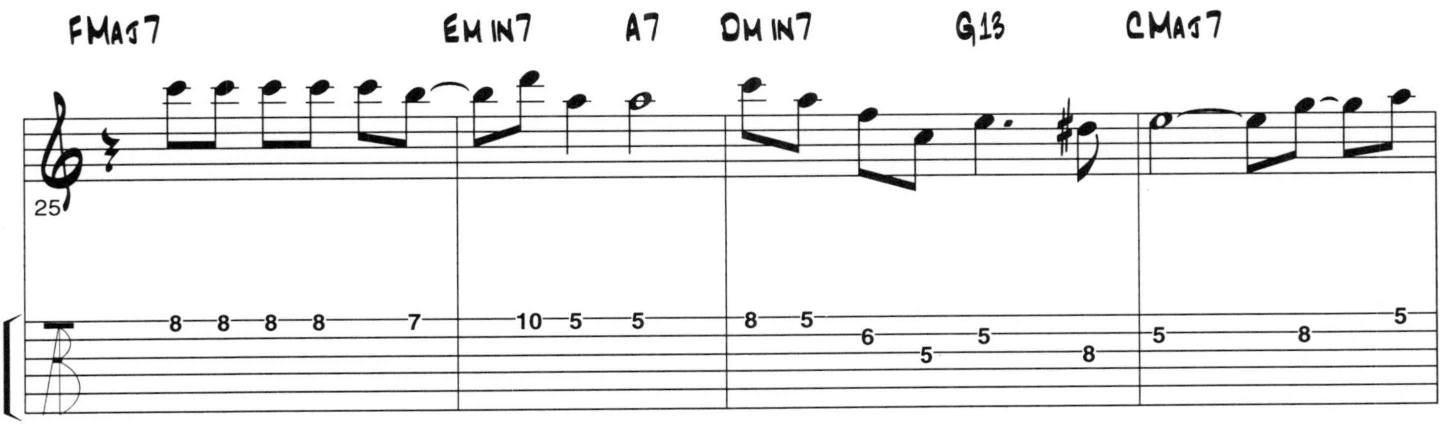
FMAJ7
EMIN7
A7
DMIN7
G13
CMAJ7
25

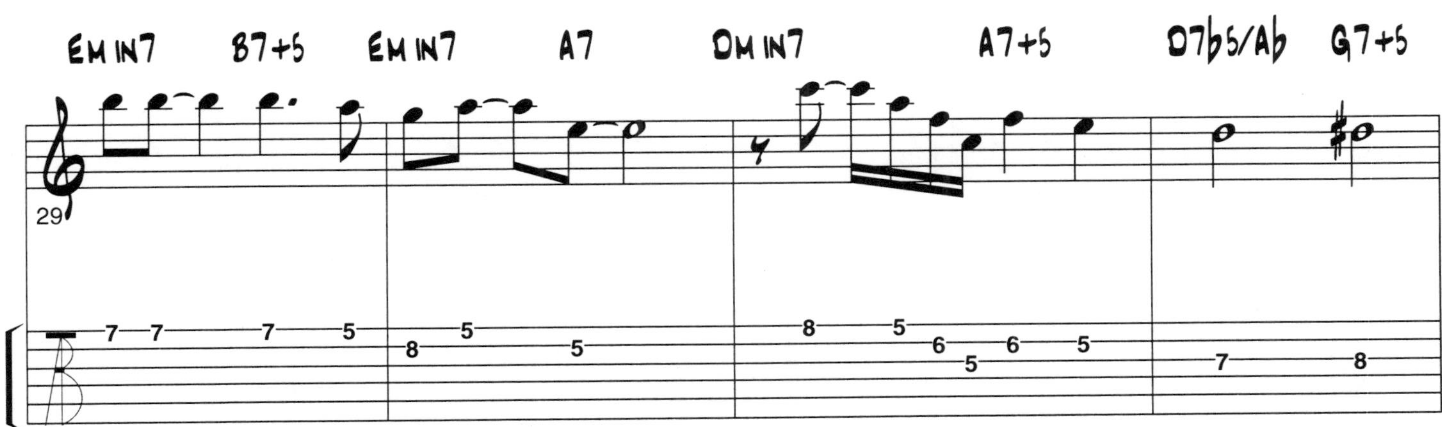
EMIN7
B7+5
EMIN7
A7
DMIN7
A7+5
D7♭5/A♭
G7+5
29

CMAJ7
G9SUS
G9
CMAJ7
G7SUS
33

F#MIN7b5
F13
EMIN7
A7+5
D7b5/Ab
G13b9
37

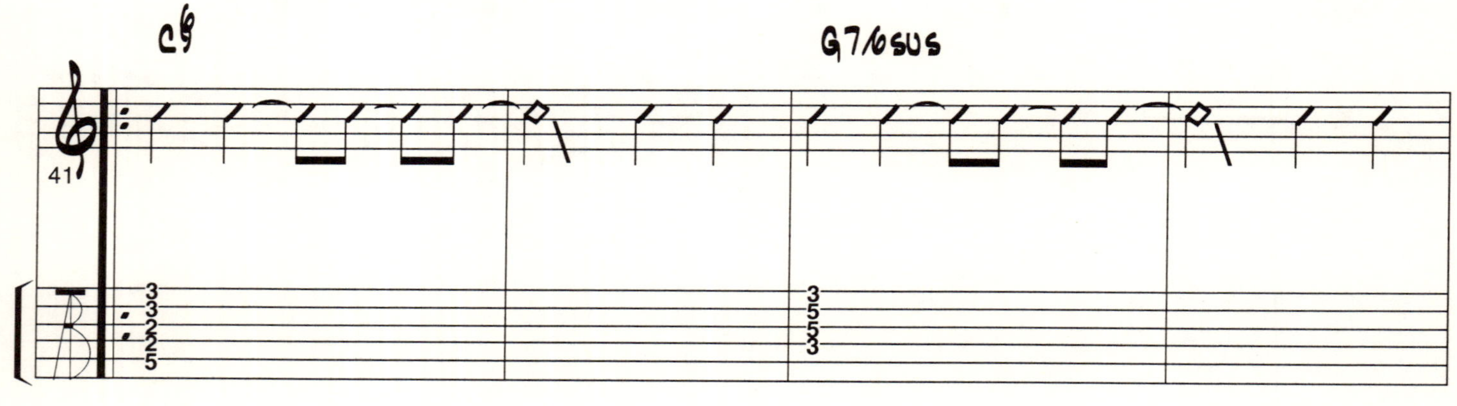
C6/9
G7/6SUS
41

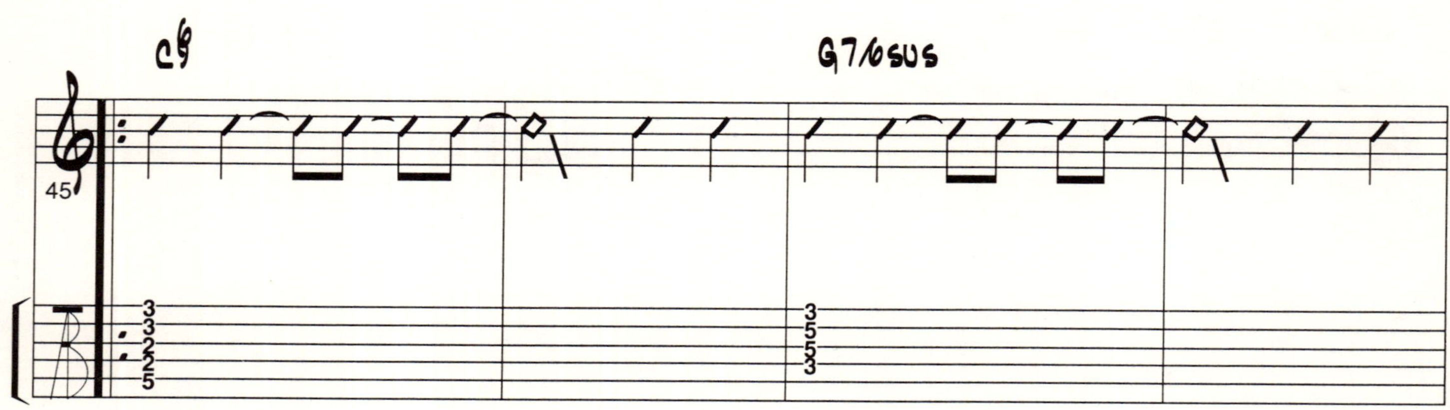
C6/9
G7/6SUS
45

THE BEACH AT IPANEMA (SOLO)
JACK JEZZRO
CMAJ7
G9SUS G9
CMAJ7
G7SUS
CMAJ7
G9SUS G9
CMAJ7
GMIN7
C7♭5/G♭
FMAJ7
FMIN7
EMIN7
AMIN7
DMIN7
D7♭5
G13♭9

MIDNIGHT IN RIO

JACK JEZZRO

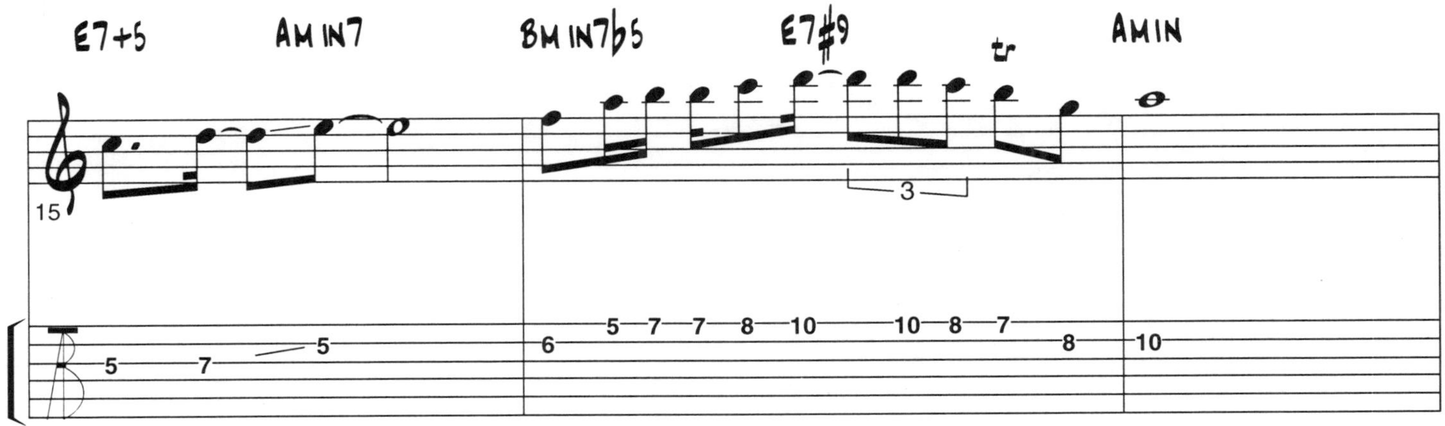
E7+5 AMIN7 BMIN7♭5 E7♯9 AMIN
15
3

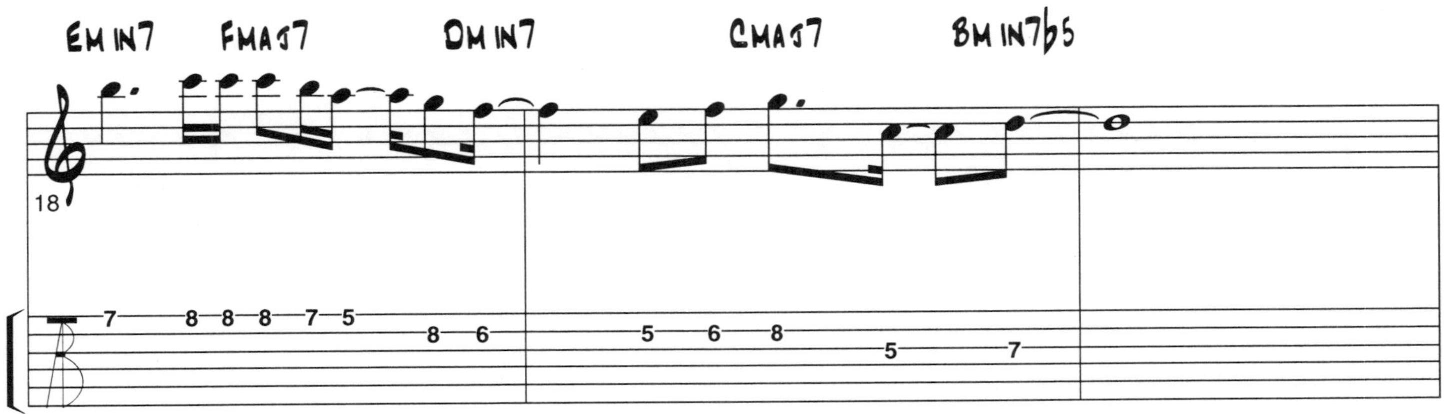
EMIN7 FMAJ7 DMIN7 CMAJ7 BMIN7♭5
18

DMIN7 CMAJ7 BMIN7♭5 E7♯9
21

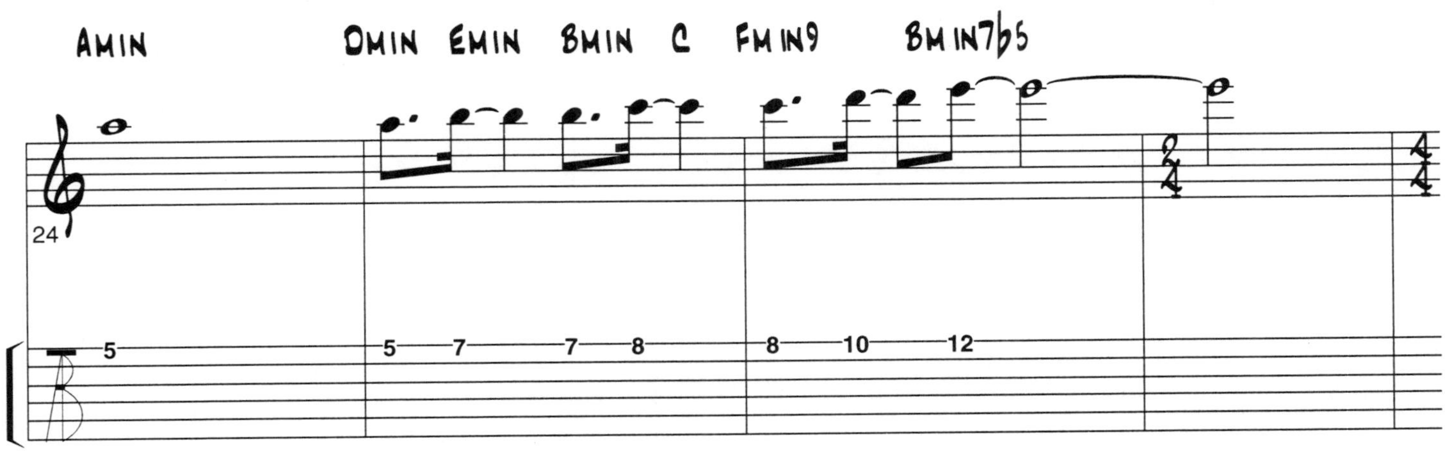
AMIN DMIN EMIN BMIN C FMIN9 BMIN7♭5
24

BMIN7♭5
E7#9
Solos (repeat 3 times)
AMIN
GMIN7
C7♭9
FMAJ7
EMIN7
AMIN7
FMAJ7
Positions for chords:
BMIN7♭5
E7#9
AMIN
E7#9#5
AMIN
GMIN7
C7♭9
FMAJ7
EMIN7
AMIN7
FMAJ7
BMIN7♭5
E7#9

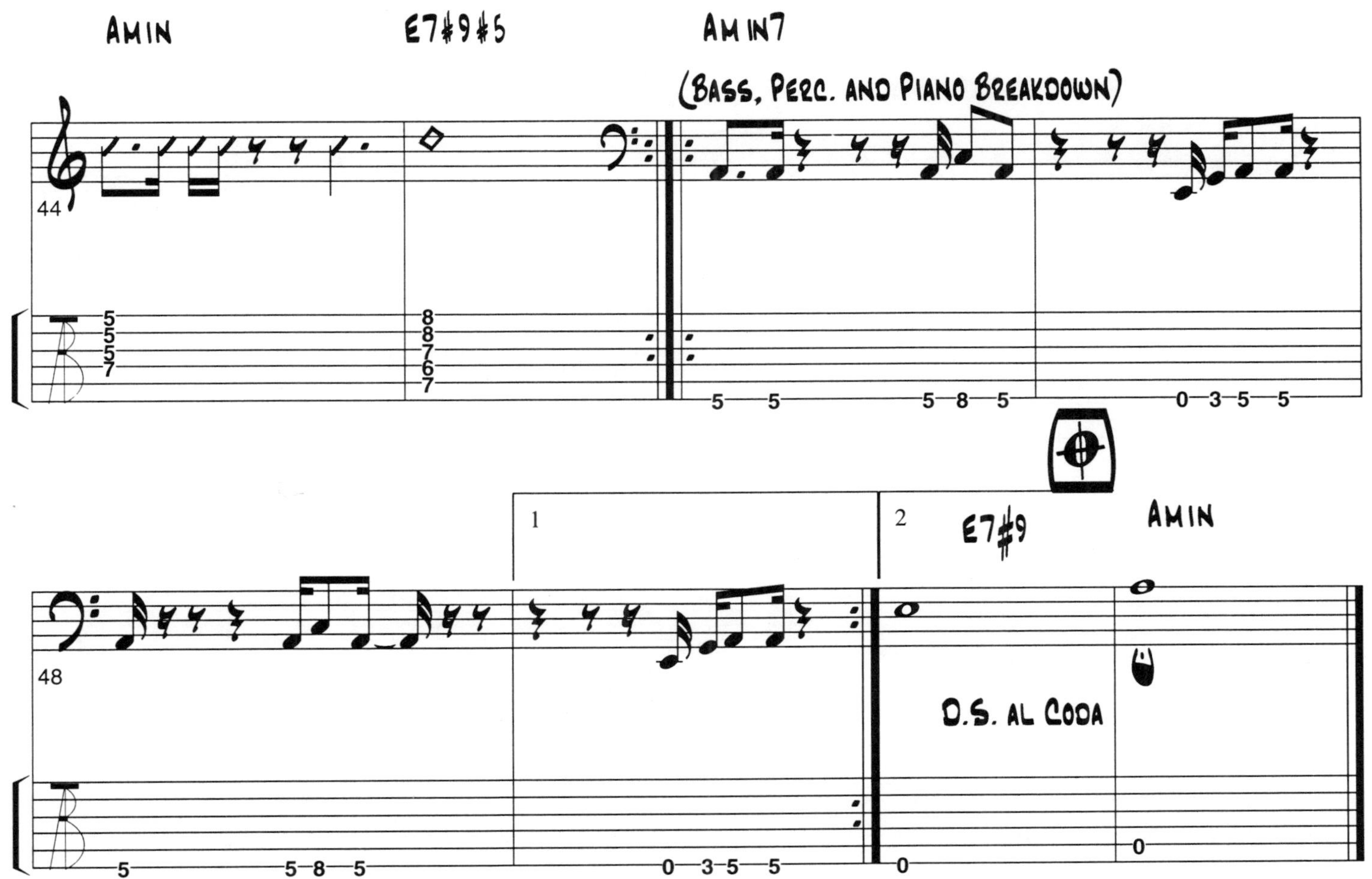
AMIN
E7#9#5
AMIN7
(BASS, PERC. AND PIANO BREAKDOWN)
44
48
1
2
E7#9
AMIN
D.S. AL CODA

Midnight in Rio (solo)

Jack Jezzro

(at 00:58; note change to cut-time)

AMIN7
E7#9
13

AMIN
16

GMIN7
C7♭9
FMAJ7
19

EMIN7
AMIN7
22

FMAJ7
B11
BMIN7♭5
25
5
5
5 6 8
5 6 8
12
10
11
9
12
10
11
9
10
12
10
10
9

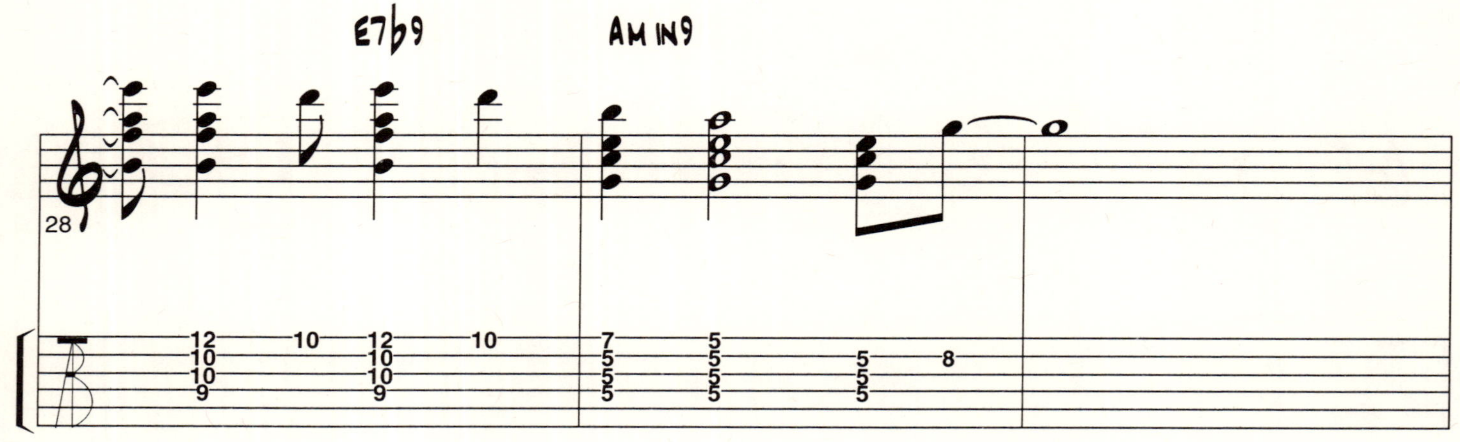
E7♭9
AMIN9
28
12
10
10
9
10
12
10
10
9
10
7
5
5
5
5
5
5
5
5
5
5
8

BMIN7♭5
E7♯9
AMIN
(PICKUP TO PIANO SOLO)
31
0 7 0 5 0
8 6 5 7 5

CONCLUSION

Music and guitar, when taken seriously, are lifetime studies not for the faint of heart. Great jazz guitarists, whether Pat Metheny, Wes Montgomery or Django Reinhardt, don't just fall fully-formed off the turnip truck or take some kind of magic pills. Anyone who can play this kind of music well works like crazy to get there, no matter how talented they are. And as a student of the music, you have the priceless opportunity to learn from the work done by previous generations of guitarists. By working with this book of Jack Jezzro's original compositions and improvisations, you are becoming a more mature musician, capable of realizing your own concepts and chops at a much higher level than before. Congratulations!

LENNY CARLSON

About the Author

Diversity best describes the artistry of guitarist, bassist, and producer Jack Jezzro. His recordings and productions have sold well into the millions, and he surely ranks high in formal education, knowledge of his instrument, and sheer musicality. But even more than that, Jezzro has a style and taste that are all his own–qualities that are a breath of fresh air to the music of today and qualities that breathe new life into the music of yesterday.

The Early Years

Jazz is a natural expression for this West Virginia native, who seems to have been born musical. Jack Jezzro grew up in the small town of Rivesville, starting on piano and accordion when he was very young. His remarkable skill at simultaneously fingering melody and chord changes on guitar came naturally to him as a young listener. "I had a stack of Chet Atkins records, and that's how I learned to play," Jezzro reports. " As a kid, I'd want to play all the parts. I'd listen to a tune by James Taylor, The Doobie Brothers, Simon & Garfunkel, or whomever. I'd play the bass part, the piano, the vocal–and I'd want to do it all right there on the guitar.

Education

For his bass-playing, Jezzro earned a scholarship to West Virginia University in nearby Morgantown. By 1978, Jack knew that if he wanted to become a professional, it was time to move on. So he took the year off from school and began playing in the Charleston Sypmphony Orchestra (CSO).

After a year with CSO, Jezzro won a scholarship and sailed into the sophistication of the prestigious Eastman School of Music in Rochester, New York. While a student at Eastmen, he won an audition for and subsequently played in the Rochester Philharmonic Orchestra for two years. Meanwhile, he continued devleoping a a guitarist by absorbing the sounds of George Benson, Joe Pass, and Jim Hall. After graduation, "it was either New York, Nashville, or Los Angeles, and Nashville felt more like home" where he lande a job with the Nashville Symphony Orchestra and began breaking into the studio scene.

The Jezzro Style

His latest guitar projects combine those elusive qualities instantly recognized when you hear them–discrimination, polish, grace, and artistry. In addition to sheer taste, another element of Jezzro's unique style is that he's a contrpuntal guitarist, integrating chordal harmony and melodies into one distinct sound–clean, lucid, and smooth–often performing on a nylon-string guitar.

Credits

Jezzro has nearly 200 albums to his production credit. He received a Grammy nomination for *A Day's Journey* and six Dove Award nominations for producing artists such as Brentwood Jazz Quartet and saxophonist Sam Levine. He produced the multi-platinum selling *Smoky Mountain Hymns* recordings, one of which also received a Dove Award nomination. Additionally, *The Frank Sinatra Collection* by Beegie Adair, produced by Jack Jezzro, won a Nashville Music Award for "Jazz Album of the Year." His projects have collectively sold nearly 10 million copies worldwide and feature a variety of styles including Jazz, Latin, Country, New Age, Folk, World, Gospel, Fifties, and Pop.

As an internationally acclaimed guitarists and composer, his music has been heard regularly on jazz radio stations all over the world. He has been a special guest on America's voice to the World's "Jazz Vibrations" radio show, a program broadcast to over 100 million listeners. His recordings have been heard in numerous television shows, network specials and movies, such as the 1996 Summer Olympics, *Friends*, *Entertainment Tonight*, *J-A-G*, *A&E Biography*, *Access Hollywood*, *E! True Hollywood Story*, *Martha Stewart Living*, *Honey, I Shrunk the Kids*, and more.

He has served as producer and featured performer on a full-length recording for Walt Disney Records entitled *Instrumental Impressions*. Jack has also authored books containing some of his original compostions for Mel Bay Publications, Inc. Jack Jezzro's production experience has catapulted him to become one of Nashville's premiere instrumental music producers.

About the Transcriber

Lenny Carlson has authored numerous books of guitar transcriptions and analysis for Mel Bay and other publishing companies. His most recent books are *Jeff Linsky: Latin Guitar Jazz* (Mel Bay, 2001), *Jack Jezzro: Acoustic Dreams* (Mel Bay, 1998) and *John Jackson: Don't Let Your Deal Go Down* (Arhoolie/Mel Bay, 1998) Artists included in his list of titles include blues pioneers John Lee Hooker, Lonnie Johnson and Willie Dixon, rocker Neil Young, Bahamian folk guitarist Joseph Spence and classical guitarist Stevan Pasero. He has written articles for *Acoustic Guitar* and *Fingerstyle Guitar* magazines.

An accomplished jazz guitarist, Lenny is also an award-winning composer and arranger who has produced two albums of his original music. A selection from the second album,

In the Mud, was nominated for a Grammy as Best Jazz Instrumental Composition. One of his arrangements is featured on *Noel Noel*, a Christmas, 1996 CD by the Camilli String Quartet on the Sugo label. He designed music and sound effects for video games in the early 1980s and has since composed for videos and films. He is currently arranging and performing as accompanist for jazz/pop vocalist Millicent Wood. Their first CD will be released in late Fall, 2001.

Lenny Carlson received a Master's Degree in Music Performance from Portland State University in Oregon, and is on the Music Faculties of City College of San Francisco and San Francisco State University's Music/Recording Industry Program. A native of Los Angeles, he now lives in San Francisco with his wife and two daughters.

EXCELLENCE IN MUSIC
MEL BAY®
Since 1947